In My Own Words

A NOTE FROM THE PUBLISHER

Elizabeth Clare Prophet retired in 1999 for health reasons.
Summit University Press acknowledges her extraordinary legacy,
and all profits from the sale of *In My Own Words* will go to
support her health-care needs for as long as necessary.

ELIZABETH CLARE PROPHET

In My Own Words
Memoirs of a
Twentieth-Century Mystic

SUMMIT UNIVERSITY ❧ PRESS®
Gardiner, Montana

Contents

Contents

Preface

WHEN ELIZABETH CLARE PROPHET was working on her biography, she said that one of her goals was for people "to know me spiritually and humanly." Both aspects of her life are here. She faced the same issues that everyone deals with—family, joys and sorrows, school and relationships, college and career choices. But through all of this runs the deep current of a spiritual quest that was the central purpose of her life.

In My Own Words tells the story of the early years of Mrs. Prophet's journey, her first twenty-two years, which were marked by an unusual dedication to the search for God. The seeds of the extraordinary life that was about to unfold are evident.

Mrs. Prophet went on to become one of the most well-known female spiritual leaders of the twentieth century. She appeared on *Nightline, Larry King Live* and hundreds of television and radio shows around the world. For almost three decades she led The Summit Lighthouse, a worldwide spiritual movement founded by her late husband Mark L. Prophet. She traveled to more than thirty countries and published more than fifty books to deliver her message. She is known to thousands as their spiritual teacher.

Yet even with all of her accomplishments, Mrs. Prophet was never interested in attention or fame. For her, it was the message that was important, and she was simply the messenger. Her concern was always for the spiritual progress of those she taught. If she spoke about herself, it was so that others might learn from her experiences and apply those lessons, often hard-won, to their own lives.

THIS BOOK HAS its origins in 1991, when Mrs. Prophet and members of her editorial staff first began working on it. Their research and writing continued over the next few years, but the book was not completed at that time.

About half of this present volume is drawn from Mrs. Prophet's original writing for the project. The remainder had been completed only in outline form, and the writing had not yet begun. That outline has been filled in by material compiled from her many published and unpublished lectures and interviews. The resulting memoir provides a rare insight into the life of a renowned twentieth-century mystic.

Thomas Merton once wrote: "The spiritual anguish of man has no cure but mysticism." If so, then perhaps we all have something important to learn from the mystic in our midst. In the story of her life, each of us may find a measure of inspiration for our own spiritual journey.

THE EDITORS

ELIZABETH CLARE WULF, AGE 4

1

The Heart of a Child

MY HEART WAS the heart of a child. I was innocent. I trusted. My soul knew no bounds. I had no sense of beginnings or endings. Birth and death were artificial demarcations. I had always existed in God. The infinite past and the infinite future were mine, and mine to enter at will. I thought I had come from a distant star.

The heavens were my playground, yet I was content in spaces defined. My play yard. My sandbox. My toy chest. My precious dolls. The rock garden my father built with a waterfall and fountains, a goldfish pond, water lilies, frogs croaking and birds darting to and fro, flowering periwinkle that I would sit upon, thinking it was my very own seat, and other flowers taller than I. The white picket grape arbor, with built-in benches, laden with concord and green grapes. Apple, peach and cherry trees, raspberries, blackberries, strawberries, gooseberries and red currants. These were the first sights and sounds I knew.

I was one and two and three, knowing the smells of springtime—the new grass, the trees budding, the lilac blossoms, the sprays of forsythia a maze of yellow, the dogwood, apple and cherry blossoms, the salt air from the sea and the river. Then the heavy heat of summer and hurricanes that put out the lights and tore down trees. The harvests of fall and the burning leaves, Thanksgiving and all the trimmings. And soon the cold winters with snowflakes on my cheeks, snowmen, and Christmas lights on a fresh tree cut from our land.

Childhood days were long and gradually the seasons passed. I observed their comings and their goings with delight and marveled at the ever-new wonder of life around me. Joy was in my heart. I understood the cosmic cycles. I knew that I was I and not another. I sensed the infinite in my finite world with its boundaries of squares, circles, triangles and lines, and clocks, times and schedules.

Sunbeams filtering through the massive silver maple outside my window pried open my eyes each morning. Every day I was born again to a new adventure in this life, in this plane, in this karmic circumstance. I was eager for the challenge.

As I peered through the coordinates of heaven and earth, and my playpen, I was bathed in the golden glow of the sun. It was my reality. I took for granted the gentle presence that was always with me through my darkest days and trials untold. It seemed to be a bridge from the nuts and bolts of my human existence to the timeless, spaceless, dimensionless realm from which I had come. It was the sheer gladness of the sun. And my child smile shone from the Source of Life I felt within me as well as without.

The beauty of God was never far from my mind or heart. And life was a continuum of that beauty—I had always believed that I had always been and always would be. Each day I was on a mission of self-discovery. I had to know who I was, where I had come from, and where I was going.

The quest for meaning brought on the endless "Why?" followed by questions that few or none could answer. Neighbors, parents, friends and teachers alike became exasperated with my whys. But by and by, as my life and mission unfolded, God answered every one of my childlike questions, and he revealed to me the mysteries of the kingdom in his good time. Can we not, we who seek his kingdom, say with Saint Paul, "When I was a child, I spake as a child, I understood as a child, I thought as a child.... Now we see through a glass darkly; but then face to face: now I know in part; but then shall I know even as also I am known."[1]

As I look back, I see that my mission was a seed planted in my soul by the Great Sower of the seed of life. It was a seed taken from my Tree of Life and sealed until the cycles of its gestation should commence according to the timetable of my Father-Mother God.

AT BIRTH AND in early years, I retained some conscious awareness of the realms of light from which I had descended into my mother's womb, entering the body prepared for me in this life. But as with all children, the memory faded as the soft spot at the crown closed over.

Above in the heaven-world, my soul could soar at night while my body slept in my frilly pink-and-white bassinet. Unencumbered by the limitations of my developing brain and body, I journeyed in the etheric envelope and the astral sheath, as is common in soul travel. On inner planes I knew my reason for being. I was a free spirit—neither child nor adult, but an evolving part of God. The zeal of my mission was upon me, and I served with angels and advanced souls to prepare the way for its fulfillment on earth in this life.

I knew before birth that I was yet burdened by karma. And I knew that the circumstances of my life would offer me the supreme opportunity to complete the balancing of my karma in this embodiment and to do so through the very mission itself. Therefore on inner planes I worked tirelessly with the saints, the Eastern adepts and the angels to prepare for that calling.

THE BUDDING AND sprouting of the seed of a mission depends upon the care that is given to the seed and to the soil in which it is planted. Unless emotional and physical needs are met, child-man may miss the mission for a lifetime or several. Unless the mental stimulus is there from conception, child-man may not bring back from his Tree of Life fruits needed for soul nourishment. Mental stimulus is necessary so that the seed might be quickened in the fertile soil of memory, mind, desire—those elements that continue with us but must be re-anchored in the physical sheaths of consciousness with each new birth.

Yes, we carry our past with us, but its links to the outer personality must be fixed anew. When parents, teachers, educators, pastors, friends and relatives all contribute to the proper milieu for the child, then the mission can be accomplished. When karma barricades the soul and those responsible for the soul are irresponsible, the mission can be lost.

Every newborn arrives with the bag and baggage of positive and negative karma that must be balanced and that will be brought into play in this life. Every newborn comes with a psychology carried over from many past lives. This psychology is reflected in his astrological birth chart, which outlines both positive and negative karma.

The positive momentums, talents and attainments will afford the child wind in his sails and a safe passage if he will maximize them. These talents must not be buried, neither by himself nor by his parents. They are his to multiply; and if he does so, he may experience the abundant life that Jesus promised.

The negative karma recorded in the birth chart requires responsibility and resolution, readiness for hard work and joyfulness in the labor of the Lord's vineyard. The challenges and initiations that will come can all be met if he will enter the path of discipleship under Jesus Christ, Gautama Buddha, a saint, an ascended master[2] or even a great teacher on earth. Wise are the parents who teach their children to obey the laws of God and man and to maintain a humble and merciful heart. Wise are they who take them on their knee and teach them the Ten Commandments, the Golden Rule and the Great Commandment.[3]

Because God has given the gift of free will, no mission is guaranteed. Each one must nurture the seed that God has planted in the garden of the soul. Until the child can accomplish this on his own, his parents, family life, school and the schoolyard, the neighborhood and its influences may be a daily impingement on the soul and the soul's receptivity to the inner calling—heard from above but not yet articulated in thought, in feeling or in words.

Yes, both the soul and the mission are fragile. Parents and teachers who know this will surround the children entrusted to their care with positive reinforcement of the signs of their destiny and with a spirit that lets them know that it is possible to overcome every obstacle in life—with God.

THE DEEP DESIRE to be who I am in God has been with me since my earliest moments, as time and limitation began to be clocked in cycles of feedings, my going out and coming into my body, being in my crib, my house, my carriage—as the days turned into nights and the nights turned into days.

When I awakened in the morning in my baby body, I awakened to wet diapers, an empty stomach and my own crying for my bottle, my mommy and my daddy. But I retained the sense of the will to be, of determination, the desire to drink the cup of life, all of it. To know God, to find him, to commune with him as he might reveal himself to me and talk with me—this was my longing in my early years.

A baby can think these thoughts because the mind of the child is the mind of God. Our minds are but extensions of the one universal Mind. The new body, brain and central nervous system are means through which the mind of God communicates in outer self-awareness.

Make no mistake, the child you hold in your arms has the cumulative awareness of his immediate past life or even many past lives, depending on his or her level of soul development. At the subconscious level, the soul knows all things past, present and future of her existence.

Advanced souls come "trailing clouds of glory," as Wordsworth wrote, descending from the heaven-world for another round of service. His "Ode: Intimations of Immortality" tells the cycles of their coming:

> Our birth is but a sleep and a forgetting:
> The Soul that rises with us, our life's Star,
> Hath had elsewhere its setting,
> And cometh from afar:
> Not in entire forgetfulness,

And not in utter nakedness,
But trailing clouds of glory do we come
From God, who is our home:
Heaven lies about us in our infancy!
Shades of the prison-house begin to close
Upon the growing Boy.
But he beholds the light, and whence it flows,
He sees it in his joy;
The Youth, who daily farther from the east
Must travel, still is Nature's priest,
And by the vision splendid
Is on his way attended;
At length the Man perceives it die away,
And fade into the light of common day.

Souls who have lived on the astral plane[4] between lifetimes through numerous sequences of birth and death carry momentums of lower vibrations and desires. Even so, their self-recognition is there at the subconscious level, though they may not fully come to know who and what manner of lifestream they are until well after they have reached adulthood, and sometimes not at all in this life. For to be given the records of one's past and the knowledge of who one has been, one must desire to know, to take responsibility for one's actions, and to change.

2

Birth

MY LIFE HAS been marked by miracles of divine as well as human intercession. My birth was no exception, and it was a remarkable beginning.

I was the only child born to Hans Wilhelm Wulf and Fridy Enkerli Wulf, near Red Bank, New Jersey, one of the many small towns that dot the eastern shore south of New York City. I arrived on April 8, 1939, at Monmouth Memorial Hospital in Long Branch.

The doctor hospitalized my mother two to three weeks before my due date. Her X-rays showed I was normal and in the correct position, but he gave her injections daily to hasten the delivery. Then on Friday, April 7, he informed Mother that I would be born the next morning, and he explained the planned procedure. Mother was surprised that such archaic procedures were still in use. Then, answering her question, the doctor said that 60 percent of the babies born by this method died. Mother was shocked and she cried. She was forty-two years old and I was to be her first and only child.

As soon as the doctor left, she telephoned my father and

told him what the doctor had said. It so happened that at that very moment Dr. Rullman, the foremost surgeon in that part of New Jersey, was in my father's boatyard to discuss plans for the yacht my father was building for him. Daddy told Mother that Dr. Rullman was there and that he would tell him about her situation and call her back in a few minutes.

Dr. Rullman said, "Your wife has been in the hospital in pain for two weeks. She is in no condition to make a decision. You need to take matters into your own hands. Dismiss her doctor so I can take over the case. Don't worry, Captain Wulf, I'll be over tomorrow morning and we'll deliver your baby by cesarean."

A happy and excited father-to-be called back to ask for Mother's consent. She immediately said, "Yes! Yes!" and wept for joy. As soon as Daddy took charge, the first doctor left for his Florida vacation.

Dr. Rullman scheduled the surgery for the next morning. At eight o'clock my father was in the operating room beside my mother. Later he wrote of the occasion, "In came Dr. Rullman. He saw me standing there and chased me out. 'You crazy Dutchman, get the h— out of here. I promise you, in about half an hour the nurse will come out and show you your baby.' And that is exactly what happened."

My father wrote of this moment: "I promised myself that I would always love you, love your mother, and take care of you through thick and thin to the best of my ability. Yes, there could be rainy, stormy days, but as I know from the sea, there are always sunshine days after the storm and rough seas."

The last thing my mother remembered before going into surgery was hearing the "Triumphal March" from *Aïda* playing on the radio. She said, "It gave me such courage, assurance of a triumph." Many years later when she told me the story of my birth, I knew why all of my life the mere hearing of a few strains of that piece by Verdi would summon all of my forces, all of my joy and galvanize me into action. It would quicken my heartbeat, stir my deepest feelings and transmit to me the sense of victory over all limitation, including mortality itself.

Though there were dark shadows surrounding my birth, the facts of which I was not to learn until adulthood, the light was greater and the light prevailed. And so it has been throughout my life. The golden glow of the gentle Presence has never left me.

Back in her room after surgery, my mother recalls that a nurse was carrying a newborn baby girl from room to room looking for the mother. She announced her as the "Wulf baby" but so mispronounced the name that my mother didn't recognize it. But she peeked at the baby and oohed and aahed, telling the other mothers how beautiful she was. When she finally realized that it was her own, she was quite embarrassed. The nurse affirmed, "Mrs. Wulf, you have a beautiful baby girl."

Mother wrote, "I thought she was very sweet. Her head was so well shaped, her hair was light, her eyes seemed blue. She was so precious! As I looked at her, I said, 'I hope you will be a good girl.' In a sense this was my prayer of protection for her. I reasoned that she would be protected if she did no harm."

My parents named me Elizabeth after my maternal grandmother, Elisabeth Schnyder, and Clare after Clare Weber, whose governess my mother had been. They decided to call me Betty Clare to give equal importance to both names.

The day after my birth was Easter Sunday. My mother

remembered awakening at daybreak to Easter sunrise over the Atlantic. She later wrote that her bed was near a large window with a view of the ocean. The far distant scene was painted with morning's early light. She felt the drama of Easter morning.

Then my mother's eyes fell upon a snow-white Madonna lily that someone had placed at her bedside during the night. "It looked like an apparition," she wrote. "It was saying many things to me, things I cannot translate; they were too deep." She later learned that this sign of the Resurrection had come from the chairman of the board of the hospital, General Borden, who liked to have a flower placed next to each patient. He lived in nearby Rumson and grew beautiful flowers in greenhouses tended by several gardeners.

My mother and I were in the hospital for fifteen days, and several times a day the nurses brought me to my mother for feeding. Because she was not able to nurse me, my mother thought the nurses were feeding me. But the nurses thought my mother was feeding me. So I was not fed for the first week of my life. Mother heard me cry and cry but couldn't understand why.

Dr. Rullman assumed that his partner was seeing to my case, and the first doctor was away, so I was left unattended. Again Daddy took charge and called in the best baby doctor he could find, and this doctor ordered me to be fed properly. Finally they put me on formula and I began to gain weight.

My father brought my mother and me home to their first house in Red Bank, a bungalow on Henry Street. When she walked in the door, she found a lovely surprise waiting—a bassinet, trimmed with yards of white lace over pink satin, with lovely pillows, covers, pink blankets and some baby clothes. It was a gift from Mrs. Weber, her former employer.

On my first birthday, my mother sent a bouquet of flowers to Dr. Rullman in my name in gratitude for his intercession in saving both of our lives.

3

Parents

MY FATHER WAS born on January 24, 1901, in Elmshorn, Schleswig-Holstein, Germany, to Ernest and Wilhelmina Wulf. He was christened Hans Johann Wilhelm Wulf at the local Lutheran church. Hans had three brothers—Willy, Emiel and Carl—and a half brother and sister, Ernest and Martha. They were raised with Prussian discipline by a stern father and a hardworking mother.

Hans had a brilliant mind and was at the head of his class. He was ready to graduate from school early, but because he allowed another student to copy his answers on final exams, he was held back another year. When he finally graduated, at age fourteen, his one desire was to join the German navy. World War I was under way.

Because he was underage, Hans needed his father to sign his enlistment papers. It was Christmas 1915. His father was upset over something he had done and was not speaking to him or giving him any presents. So Hans said, "I know I don't deserve any presents, but will you please just sign this paper." He had folded the paper over so his father could not see what was on it, and his father, having had his Christmas schnapps, signed without looking at it. So Hans went to officer training school and was assigned to a U-boat, the *U-63*.

About the day that he first saw his submarine, he wrote: "I was going down the dock and passing some of the most modern, large submarines, but none of them had number 63. So I finally found it, and found out that it was one of the small older types of submarines. I was taken aback, and more so when I got aboard. I had been in close quarters before, but these were really close. You could hardly move around. In many places there was only crawl space."

The *U-63* was ordered to go to Scapa Flow, a British naval base off the north of Scotland, to perform a mission. My father said they were lucky to make it out of the basin alive because of the mines, nets and other defenses around the base.

"The rest of the war was a more human war," he wrote. "We never sank any ship without warning, and we had the crew and any passengers get into lifeboats before we sank their ship. One of these sinkings was in the English Channel. We had to sink a freighter. It was a very rough sea and I was sorry for the crew and the small lifeboats because it was a long way to get to shore. We towed them, and we towed them so close to the French coast that we came under artillery fire and had to cut loose the lifeboats and get out of there in a hurry. We made it without damage to ourselves."

My father would describe the scrapes that the old submarine got into, especially after enemy ships started dropping depth charges on them. "When we had to dive or run away from somebody, we had to be very careful with our air," he wrote. "Many times I thought to myself when we were in trouble, Why did I volunteer for this service?"

After the armistice, the allies ordered the German navy

officers to clear all the mines with minesweepers, a dangerous job at first because they had to pick up the mines and take off the detonators. Later, they destroyed them with gunfire. After his duty on a minesweeper, my father returned to his original port and resigned from the German navy.

In Hamburg my father found a job on a German cargo steamer, the *Rheinbeck,* which was bound for the Russian port of Archangel. It was his ticket to see the world. From there the ship went to England and, after spending the winter in Liverpool for repairs, sailed to the West Indies and South America.

My father quit the *Rheinbeck* in San Juan, Puerto Rico, with two of his fellow German sailors. They went ashore with no money and no jobs. Thus started a slew of adventures and more voyages on cargo ships. While on a Norwegian ship, they stopped at the harbor of Maracaibo in Venezuela. They liked the town and the countryside enough that they decided to stay.

After doing menial jobs on plantations and around the town, the three Germans managed to use the little English they knew to get jobs as mechanics in the repair yards of Shell Oil. Soon Hans was working on boats, and he quickly caught the notice of the master mechanic and the head office. He was promoted to foreman of a repair shop at the port of La Salina on Lake Maracaibo, where the Shell oil wells were, and then to port captain at the Catatumbo River. The innovations he instituted and the money he saved the company prompted his bosses to give him a raise. They also sent him back to Germany for a three-month vacation.

When he returned, my father was given another post at La Salina, this time as chief of equipment in the company's main dry dock. He also got a license from the Venezuelan government that recognized him as a ship's captain.

Another three years went by and my father was ready for another furlough. By this time it was 1932 and Hitler had begun to change the country my father once knew. He wrote, "Walking through my hometown, I was uncomfortable with all these raised-arm salutes and swastika flags everywhere.... Nothing good could come out of this."

After only a month in Germany, my father left for New York City and spent the rest of his holiday there. He moved into a little hotel on 46th Street next to Broadway and saw the town, playing the part of the tourist. He even went to Niagara Falls. Soon, too soon, the holiday was over and he went back to Venezuela, where as a port captain he took the company ships between Maracaibo, Curaçao, Aruba and Trinidad.

On a visit to Port of Spain, Trinidad, Hans found a higher paying job as port captain with an American coal company. My father liked it better in Trinidad. He rented a house and hired a cook to prepare him European meals. He even joined the Port of Spain Country Club, where he met an American couple who owned two plantations in Venezuela that were in poor condition and plagued by debts. My father helped the couple pay off the debts and get the plantations running again, and in gratitude they sold him the title to one of the plantations, called Pargo.

ENTER FRIDY ENKERLI. My mother was born on September 14, 1896, in Bulle, in the canton of Fribourg, Switzerland, to Adolf Enkerli and Elisabeth Schnyder Enkerli. She was christened Frieda Enkerli in the Protestant church and grew up in Bulle. (As soon as she was old enough to have a say in the matter, she changed her name legally to Fridy. For some reason, she couldn't stand the name Frieda and would not tolerate anyone calling her that.) She had two brothers, Adolf and Werner, and three sisters, Martha, Gertrude and Marguerite.

Fridy's mother had grown up on the family farm, Uttewil, in the canton of Fribourg in the German-speaking part of Switzerland. She was the youngest of great-grandfather Schnyder's twenty-two children. His first wife died in childbirth and he married her sister, my great-grandmother. Seventeen of these children grew to maturity. They were raised in the tradition of the Swiss-German people—proud, aristocratic, talented, hard-working—and their descendants run the family farm to this day.

With all the responsibilities of a large family, this second wife, who was Elisabeth Schnyder's mother, was hard-pressed to give all of her children the attention they needed. My grandmother said that as a child she always dreamed that her mother would come and kiss her, and once she did.

My grandmother ventured into the French-speaking part of Switzerland and found the man she married, Adolf Enkerli. Adolf was French-Swiss, a butcher by trade, whose Protestant ancestors had come from Bavaria to escape persecution. He worked hard in his butcher shop but they were never well-off.

The French-Swiss are more carefree and lighthearted than the stern and disciplined German-Swiss, and Adolf was full of fun, always making his children laugh. In their relationship, Adolf was said to have the heart and Elisabeth, a stern and proud woman, the will and power. Fridy took after her father.

In Fribourg, Fridy completed normal school (teachers training) and then set out for London to make her way in the world. She was trained as a governess and tutor with other

Swiss girls and went to work for a prominent London family, the Darwin P. Rudds. After she served them for seven years, the Rudds recommended her to Orlando F. Weber of Mount Kisco, New York, one the founders of Allied Chemical. So she set sail for the United States and was employed as governess and tutor to Clare Weber. Fridy spoke flawless English in the British tradition and taught French throughout her life.

In about 1936 she was in Port of Spain on an expedition organized by Orlando F. Weber Jr., the son of her employers. He had brought the nation's leading ornithologist, Gladys Gordon Fry, and other experts to study the birds in Venezuela and Trinidad.

The expedition started out in Trinidad. One night, the party went to the Port of Spain Country Club, where the band of a German battleship was playing. The band provided much better music than the country club's usual local selections. Hans Wulf was there, seated at a table with the captain of the battleship. The captain noticed that the mademoiselle at the next table was eyeing my father and suggested that he invite her to dance.

It was a slow waltz, so they had a chance to get acquainted. With her dark, stylishly coifed hair and her glamorous clothes, Fridy cut a stunning figure, and Hans saw her as the sophisticated European woman that she was. She, too, was taken, with my father. When the evening was over, the American expedition went on its way and Hans went back to his job and life in Port of Spain. Little did they know that their paths would soon cross again.

My father had just built a motor-sailing schooner out of a lifeboat discarded from one of the ships that bought coal from his company. He had repaired the hull and installed a Ford motor and a mast for sailing. A few days after the night he met my mother, he decided that he wanted to take his boat on its first trip to Venezuela. So he got a ten-day leave from his company and headed for Pargo, on the north side of the Paria peninsula.

My father told the port authority that he was going to the Yagua plantation first, on the south side of the peninsula, owned by the American couple that had sold him Pargo. The port officials told him that some Americans were staying at Yagua and asked him to carry some mail and a package of meat for them. My father wrote about what happened next:

"I arrived at Yagua and anchored my ship as close to the beach as I could without hitting the bottom, took my shoes and socks off, and waded to the shore. I had a welcoming committee of one. From a distance, I could not establish the identity, male or female, dressed in a khaki shirt, riding britches, knee-high boots and a tropical helmet. I did not expect to see the lady I danced with in the country club in Port of Spain. But it was her—Miss Fridy Enkerli. A very friendly greeting from both sides and she seemed to be glad to see me again."

Everyone in the party—Orlando Weber, Fridy Enkerli, Mrs. Gladys Gordon Fry and Bryce Metcalf (both friends of the Webers), and two bird experts from Tobago—was glad to see Captain Wulf again. He had arrived at the right time. For not only were the Americans waiting for their meat, but they did not have a cook. Unfortunately, the Chinese cook they had hired in Trinidad had suddenly died the day before.

Hans set everything straight. He organized a funeral in the plantation cemetery, which all the Americans and laborers attended. He also found a new cook among the laborers, and after he made sure the meals were good, he announced to the party that he was going to set sail the next morning for his own plantation.

Bryce Metcalf, Fridy Enkerli and the two bird experts asked if they could come along. As the length of the Paria peninsula was divided by a mountain range and Capt. Wulf's plantation was on the north side, the trip would provide a marvelous opportunity for the bird experts to study the bird populations of both sides, which they expected to be altogether different.

Hans was glad to have the company, and they were glad to have a guide. He took them safely through the Dragon's Mouth, the only channel from the Gulf of Paria to the Caribbean Sea. But the water was so rough that he found lodging for everyone for the night at a friendly plantation and traveled through the strait the next morning, when the sea was calmer. In five hours they were at Capt. Wulf's plantation.

What the travelers saw was a beautiful ranch house with a thatched roof tucked under palm trees and flower bushes. Capt. Wulf entertained them there for seven days. They had a clean beach, decorated with palm trees, on which to lounge. In the river up the hill was a little pool that Capt. Wulf had made with rocks he had carried there. It must have been a holiday in paradise for my mother. For after returning to Yagua and the rest of the party, Capt. Wulf and Miss Enkerli announced that they were engaged to be married.

After that, Capt. Wulf took the party back to Port of Spain, and they had him as their guest at the Hotel de Paris. He showed them all around Port of Spain and took them on tours of the surrounding plantations. The days passed quickly, and when it came time for the Americans to leave, Fridy suggested that Hans move to the United States with her and that they start a new life there.

So my father got a visa to immigrate to the United States.

After selling his house, his car and his boat, he took the first passenger ship to New York City, where he had an attack of malaria. As soon as he recovered, Fridy and Hans got married.

They decided to move to Red Bank, New Jersey, because friends of Fridy, a Swiss couple named the Oeschkers, invited them to move into their large house with them. It was convenient for both couples since they shared transportation and their mutual love of Swiss cooking.

It didn't take my father long to find out about a boatyard that had gone bankrupt and was up for sale. This was his chance to fulfill his lifelong dream of building custom-designed yachts.

He established the Red Bank Marine Works on the Shrewsbury River. This was a family affair. My parents made it a corporation, and since my mother was already a U.S. citizen, she was the president. My father was the vice-president, and the former secretary for the firm, Rosie Beckenstein, was the third officer. After my father opened for business, my parents decided that it was time to settle down. So they rented a bungalow on Henry Street, our first home.

At the time my father started his business, World War II was just beginning. And although the United States did not enter the war until December 1941, people were not buying boats, either for pleasure or commercial fishing. So my father decided he would, in his words, "go to Washington and see if Uncle Sam needs some boats."

4

Early Memories

ABOUT A MONTH after my first birthday, my parents bought the house at 43 South Street. It was an eighty-year-old, two-story clapboard house with a cellar and an attic. It had been the original farmhouse in that area, and little by little other homes had been built and the streets of the town of Red Bank had filled in.

Among the early memories of my childhood are scenes in my play yard with my playmates. My surroundings were truly idyllic. My father fixed up the old tool shed as a playhouse. On the east wall he put in a beautiful stained-glass window from an old mansion that had been torn down in Rumson. The morning sun shone through the aquas, blues and purples of a clipper ship sailing on the high seas. What it conveyed to me, what I sensed (though unarticulated by my child awareness) was the depth and power of the ocean of God's being and the movement of the ship of identity across the sea of life.

Many years later, when I was twenty-two and under training by Mark L. Prophet, my late husband, he wrote down a poem for me that recalled this thoughtform of my childhood:

Onward, courage!
Then blame not the Bard
When the wind and the gale
Sweep o'er the moor
And bow down the sail,
For the ship shall move on
And the Port be obtained
If the courage be high
And the will be maintained!

Just across the garden path from my playhouse door was a white picket fence enclosing my very own play yard. Here Daddy built me a rope swing with a heavy wooden seat suspended from sturdy metal poles that formed an arch. Because the ropes were long, my friends and I could swing high. And swing we did, by the hour. There was a sandbox; a large, round, low table about a foot high for making mud pies and other concoctions; and a large box with two lids. This box alternated as the icebox for mud pies and a home for the rabbits who escaped from the Morris boys' pen next door from time to time.

Under the back window in our large, sunny kitchen, my father built me a red chest with my name on top stamped in gold and outlined in black. In that chest I kept mostly toys, blocks and some dolls and handmade doll clothes.

Father and Mother decided that there should be a map of the world over my toy chest. And so one day, at my two-year-old eye level, they put up a colorful map with the names of all the countries and capital cities in bold type. I couldn't read, so I would look at the countries, point to them and ask my mother, who would be cooking or washing dishes, "What is this country? What is that country?" No matter how many times I would ask her, she would tell me again.

Soon I had memorized all of the countries in the world. But more than that, I was developing a world awareness as I played with my blocks on the black-and-white checkered kitchen linoleum. As my mother would tell me about these countries and impart to me her knowledge of the world, I would put my finger on a country and get a sense of what it was like there, and what the people and children were like.

One Easter, a friend of my parents gave me an Easter basket with a hen and a dozen chicks. My father went to work and built an elaborate chicken house and chicken pen. Mother and I took care of the chickens for many years, collecting their eggs each morning and feeding them grain, water and leftovers. When we let the chickens out to wander in the fresh grass, they would often stray from the backyard to the front and then go next door or across the street onto the neighbors' lawns and gardens. I ran after them and shooed them back to their pen. We named the mother hen Lucy Locket and we called another one Chicken Little.

I was often making mud pies, swinging on my swing or rolling down the hill of green grass from the back door to the chicken coop. Or I'd be riding my trike or scooter up and down South Street with my best friend, Jane Petherbridge. Sometimes I was picking little weeds that choked the flowers in the rock garden or plucking the dead leaves and flowers off of the geraniums in their pots. Otherwise, I was sure to be found on the front porch with my dolls, my doll carriage, my doll beds and high chairs, and a toy stove and kitchen sink. Jane would bring over her dolls and doll carriage and we would play house by the hour.

Wisteria vines entwined themselves about the front porch roof and balustrades and had done so for decades. In the summertime, they provided shade on the sunny side of the house. Clusters of pale purple flowers tumbled from the branches. For me the scent of wisteria is a sweet scent of childhood and early "motherhood."

I took care of Trudy, my littlest doll, with her handmade dresses, nighties, and pink angora hat and coat. There was Pamela, whom I could bathe, and Gwendolyn in her knitted skirt, sweater and hat. She had beautiful golden blond hair and, like the others, eyes that opened and shut. Then there was Emily, the largest doll of all. I have no idea where she came from, but the top of her head and her hair were missing. All were loved and cared for as my very own babies. Mother and my Swiss aunts kept me supplied with the sweetest doll clothes. As Jane and I grew older, we got new dolls that could drink and wet their diapers. We could wash and set their hair and give them baths.

I had several dollhouses when I was a child. The last and the largest was built by my father, and my collection of dolls and doll furniture for it was considerable. Jane and I spent many a winter's afternoon and evening enacting all kinds of stories and plays with the families who lived in our dollhouses.

By the time I was eight years old, I was taking care of real babies around the neighborhood. It was my greatest happiness to be allowed to wheel the neighborhood babies up and down the street, feed them their lunch or supper, or care for them at the beach. By and by I was in demand as a babysitter and continued this occupation through high school as a means of earning money for clothes and college.

THEN THERE WAS Barry. He was a cross between a spitz and a fox terrier. With a long white coat and tail, caramel ears and spot on the center of his head, and a large circle of caramel on his back, he was the cutest little puppy I had ever seen.

Barry was born at the boatyard on Andy's houseboat. Andy was kind of the bum of the Shrewsbury River. My father let him tie up his boat in an out-of-the-way corner of the yard and kind of keep an eye on things. We all loved him and he lived the life he wanted to live. Each time I went down to the river I would pay him a visit. Unshaven and unkempt, he would smile and talk to me. Sometimes he would invite me aboard. It was the biggest mess I had ever seen. Open cans of half-eaten food, an old coffee pot, dirty clothes and everything just where he'd left it lie for weeks.

When the puppies were born in Andy's boat, my father picked the best of the litter and brought him home one night when I was four or five, much to my delight but not to my mother's. She was upset because she thought she would have to do all the work. But when Daddy and I assured her that we would take care of the little dog, she warmed up to him and decided he should be named Barry after the Saint Bernard dog that had lived on the family farm at Uttewil. So Barry he was. Mother had the loudest whistle, and both Barry and I would respond to her call whenever we were roaming in the neighborhood.

I immediately became Barry's master, house-trained him, fed him and took him with me everywhere. I gave him the little hand-painted wood-and-straw chair my mother had brought me from Mexico and put it next to the silver-painted radiator in the kitchen, where he would be cozy in winter and cool in summer. It remained his bed for the sixteen years of his doggie life. When he and I were both little, I wheeled him around in my doll carriage, but by and by he learned to escape.

One day Barry was hit by an old jalopy in front of our house. Daddy and I were right there, working on the front lawn. We heard him yelp in pain and turned around to see the driver speed away. Daddy picked him up and carried him to the house, where we made a little hospital bed for him. We nursed him back to health, but thereafter he had a special little three-legged walk. He favored his injured foot, which only touched the ground now and then. The walk became his mark of distinction.

Every day when I came home from school, Barry would be waiting on the front lawn. He would take giant leaps into the air and then run long circles around me the full length and breadth of the yard. He looked so funny that I would laugh and clap and cheer him on, which only made him run faster and faster.

When he got dirty, I used to give him a bath in the bathtub, but not before all was ready. First the bathroom had to be lined with all the old towels, the bathtub filled with warm soapy water and the door sealed shut. I had to hold him down while he got all scrubbed and fluffy white. Before I mastered the art of doggie bathing, the first chance he got Barry would leap out soaking wet and shake himself all over the bathroom. Then I would recapture him and put him back till he was scrubbed, deticked, deflead and thoroughly rinsed. Finally I would fluff him dry and comb him till he looked "buffle," as Mother used to say.

One day when he was about six years old, I decided that Barry needed his nails clipped and I decided that the ironing board would be a good operating table. I laid him on his back with all four paws straight up and began the procedure. Barry let out a howl like I had never heard. Needless to say, the operation was unsuccessful.

When the Eastmans' boxer moved in next door, Barry went through an identity crisis. As far as the boxer was concerned, Barry was a non-dog. The boxer would walk about his yard and ours with a disdainful air, totally ignoring Barry. Barry would bark and yip at him but to no avail. Finally one day the boxer had had enough and he put Barry in his place. After the tussle, it seemed like Barry made sure his bark wasn't so challenging.

From the day he arrived, Barry's water and food bowls were in a corner of the kitchen. I would try to make him eat his dog food but he would just stare at it mournfully. He preferred table scraps and would sit and beg at every meal, eyeing each morsel from fork to mouth. Father, Mother and I would never fail to share bits and scraps, and he would leap into the air to earn his prize.

Barry had a good heart. In the later years of my childhood, when all joy had flown from my parents' marriage and hardships set in, he was a faithful friend who brought joy to my life and comforted both of my parents.

I was away at college when Daddy wrote to tell me that Barry was ailing. He slept most of the time but made an effort to go outside for his needs so he wouldn't be a burden. Barry passed on peacefully, and my father and mother buried him in a little box under a tall fir tree and erected a little white cross over his grave. Thus ended the happy days of a faithful friend who gave a truly unconditional love to each member of our family.

5

Neighbors

WHEN REMINISCING ABOUT the move to 43 South Street, Mother could hardly begin without mentioning our neighbors, the Morrises, who befriended our family the very day we arrived: "Our next-door neighbors to the south were Greek. There were five children, the oldest Taki, then George, Angie, Stephen and Elvira. All except Elvira had been born in Red Bank. Their father, Mr. Morris, took the family back to Greece in 1934, his wife being so homesick. They stayed until the end of 1939....

"We hadn't been moved in for a day when our new neighbors befriended us! What a happy life we were to have as next-door neighbors! The more children there are, the greater the love is and the more there is of it. Elvira was so affectionate and had a great, quiet smile. I sometimes found her early in the morning sitting on the back step. She was waiting for the baby....

"Dear, sweet Betty Clare was a very shy baby and her complexion was rather pale. Angie was very motherly to her. I was so thankful for the many evenings she came over to our house as Hans and I sat down to dinner in the kitchen. Betty Clare could be heard crying upstairs in her crib. It was still daylight and too early to go to sleep. Her tears would not stop.

"Many times when I ran up to check, I found Angie already there comforting the little one. During the day I put the playpen on the lawn outside the kitchen window so I could see her easily while working. The little darling did not like to be there without anyone and she cried and cried. This stopped as soon as her littlest friend Elvira came running to pull her out of the pen."

I was always welcome next door at the Morrises' and they were welcome at our house too. They gave me a different kind of family life than I had at home. Both families shaped me, my future and my worldview. I delighted in being the baby of five older brothers and sisters who loved me and took care of me. It was in their house that I learned to walk, while my mother was on a trip to Mexico with Mrs. Weber.

When my mother was serving my father supper, he didn't want to be disturbed by my crying. So Angie and Elvira would tiptoe in the front door and up the stairs and pull me out of my crib. Then, with one of them carrying me in their arms, they tiptoed back out again and ran to their house to amuse me and play with me to my heart's content.

Sometimes Mother would get the family car for the day and take us all to the beach, or her friend Agnes Schwenker would round us up and take us, along with her sons Carl and John. I could never get enough of the sun and sand and sea. If it had been up to me, I would have spent all day every day there. In the summertime my father's customers and friends would sometimes invite me, Mother, Angie and Elvira to go for rides on the Shrewsbury River on their Sea-Wulf skiffs.

And summer was also a time for baseball on South Street. I played whenever Daddy would let me off from my garden work.

At times the Morris boys teased me and scared me, pretending to be the boogeyman, especially Georgie. I remember, too, how we used to huddle around the radio and listen to *The Lone Ranger* and other adventure programs. Once I went with the whole family to the drive-in theater to see *Francis the Talking Mule*. I thought it was the funniest movie I'd ever seen. It reminded me of the Bible story of Balaam and the ass that talked to him.

When I entered junior high, the Morris children taught me ballroom dancing in their indoor sun porch. First was the Foxtrot. Elvira would say, "Slow, slow, quick, quick, slow; slow, slow, quick, quick" as I stepped to the time of the music. They had a Victrola and played the popular music of the early fifties. My favorite songs were "Begin the Beguine" and "Because of You." We also listened to Glenn Miller and the big bands of the forties. Then came the waltz, the tango, the rumba and the jitterbug, and even the Charleston. Later, in high school, I used to teach my boyfriends how to dance in our living room with my own records and record player. Like the sea and the salt air, dancing was in my blood, and it has been a happy recreation ever since.

Mrs. Morris was devout in her practice of the Greek Orthodox religion. I used to follow her around the house while she was saying prayers and carrying frankincense from room to room. In the bedrooms she had Eastern paintings of Mary and Jesus adorned with crosses made of palms from Palm Sunday. I loved the religious art and the ritual. Mrs. Morris believed that the Blessed Virgin and the angels protected and cared for her children—and I knew they did too.

I remember how Stephen Morris taught me to ride my first two-wheel bike up and down South Street. It seemed I would never get the hang of it, and patient "Saint Stephen" would run up and down the street with me night after night. One day I made up my mind that this was the day I was going to ride my bike. I prayed to God to help me and asked him to be my partner and ride with me. Then I thought, "If God is going to be my partner, why don't I just ask him to ride my bike *through* me." So I did. I said, "God, please ride my bike with me and through me, and I'll ride it too." And when I made up my mind to do it, with God, I got on my bike and rode. I was riding when Stephen came home and saw me. He was so happy and I was too.

I remembered the Bible verse, "With men it is impossible, but not with God: for with God all things are possible."[5] After that I determined to prove this law every day of my life. I tested it again and again and found that if I did my part, God would do his. But if I didn't take the necessary, practical human footsteps, this law would not work for me. I had to meet God at least halfway, and then some. I had to do all that was humanly possible. I had to stretch the limits of my ability. My reach had to exceed my grasp. Then, and only then, would God enter and supply the power and the grace for each new challenge and achievement.

The key word, I found, was *with*—"*With* God all things are possible." This meant that working with him and being on his team, I could accomplish his will, which I would make my own. But the sealing of my understanding was Jesus' statement "My Father worketh hitherto, and I work."[6] This was true partnership. This is what I wanted my life to be—a partnership with God. And I went after it.

6

Ellis Island

IT WAS THE night of March 3, 1942, and I would be three years old in one month. My parents were seated at the dining room table entertaining guests who had been with them on the expedition to Venezuela. The doorbell rang and I ran to answer it.

Since we had moved into the house, my father had brought oak paneling and chandeliers from the old mansion in Rumson, and he had spent nine months remodeling the dining room and library. We now had a fireplace, bookshelves, cabinets with leaded windows, china and liquor closets, and drawers for linen and flatware. And just the day before, my father had installed a new front door, the front door I was now opening.

Three tall men stood there. I was so small and they were so tall. Who were they? What did they want? They asked to see my father and I ran to get him.

There were two FBI agents and the chief of police. They had come to take my father away. He was an enemy alien, they said. They searched the house and took his German cameras, binoculars and other personal items. And they sent him to Ellis Island. He was not an American citizen; he was a German citizen and we were at war with Germany.

Before my father was taken to Ellis Island, the Department of the Navy had just handed him a contract to build sea skiffs that would be used in the war as landing craft. He suspected that one of his competitors on the Shrewsbury River had reported him to the authorities as a Nazi spy. In fact, my father's suspicions caused a lifelong rivalry and animosity between him and this man.

In a letter my mother wrote to my father the next day, she said:

> It seems an eternity since last evening from dinnertime on. I was too stunned to let my emotions run away when you left, but later through the night and this morning I was in tears....
>
> I wonder whether you had a hearing today. I hope so. Do you want me to send your overcoat? It must be cold there and lots of wind. Betty Clare is with Angie in her carriage; she loves to be wheeled! She asked for Daddy many times and made sand pies for you. I told her you had gone away to get some more wood for her playhouse and fence....
>
> Mr. Schwartz told me that all aliens in our territory were looked after last night. So it is not a personal reflection on you. This is little help in your predicament; anyway it's something....

The days turned into weeks. My mother made weekly trips to Ellis Island to visit my father and left me at home with her friends Mrs. Black and her daughter, Olga. They didn't have much of the things of this world but they sure had a lot of love. I remember that I felt their love and they comforted me through the long hours of my mother's absence and my father being away.

On April 17, six weeks after the FBI had come to get my father, he was finally released from Ellis Island. Witnesses who knew him well testified in a hearing that he was an upright citizen and he was not conspiring with the Nazi enemy. Although my father was allowed to leave Ellis Island, he was put on parole on the condition that he would not leave the town of Red Bank. The army and navy even got him to build more boats, but the parole wasn't lifted until after the war.

Whenever my father spoke of the day when he was released from Ellis Island, he would repeat these words—words that he wanted burned in my memory forever: "Betty Clare, I don't want you to forget that the people who gave me my freedom by coming forward to witness for me were Jews. There was Rosie Beckenstein, my secretary, and Murray Schwartz, my attorney. Even though I was German and accused of being a Nazi (which, as you know, I never was), they were willing to stand up for me. And because of their kindness, I was able to come home to you and your mother before the war was over. And after the war they never held against me what the Nazis did to the Jews.

"I want you to remember to be a friend to all Jews and anyone you see being persecuted. There's good in everyone, just as no one is without fault. But no one should have to suffer because of their nationality, their race or their religion. And you see to it that you live and let live and help people who need your help."

No, Daddy, I never forgot the night those three men came

to the door, and I will never forget who saved you when there was no one else to stick up for you. When I would hear kids at school talking about Jews, Negroes and East European immigrants, I would remember. All my friends were welcome at our house. We understood what it was like to be singled out and ostracized through guilt by association. And I learned my first lesson at the age of three about the price of liberty, the abuse of power and the exigencies of war.

7

The War

WORLD WAR II began when Hitler's armies invaded Poland on September 1, 1939. Against the backdrop of this mundane astrology, I had made my entrance on the world scene.

It was the century of war. To me, the war was not far across the sea. It was in my hometown. It was at our house. We lived near Fort Monmouth, an army base. During the war German submarines were patrolling off the Jersey shore.

I was not yet three when we started having air-raid drills. During a drill all the lights in the house had to be out. Air-raid wardens would go up and down the blocks checking to see if everyone's lights were out. On a number of occasions my mother used a flashlight or lit a candle, and very quickly there would be a loud knock at the door. The warden would inform her that he could see the light through a crack in the drapes.

Every day at noon the air-raid siren would sound. The blast was so loud that you could hear it from one end of the town to the other. The air-raid siren was also the fire siren. Whenever there was a fire, the siren would go off a certain number of times, signifying what area of town the fire was in. As soon as the siren went off, everyone would be still and count the number of blasts, then check the fire alarm list to see where the fire was. When the fire alarm went off at night, our family always checked to see if the fire was in the area of our home or my father's business. When it was the latter, my father would tear off in his car to check if everything was OK. Once there actually was a fire in the paint shed at the boatyard, but it was quickly put out.

One way people could help the war effort was to have their own "victory garden" and grow their own food. Our garden, always full of vegetables and fruits, was a big production.

When my father and mother were galvanized in the cause of the war, they rose to levels of heroism. I saw their best side and understood through the eyes of my immigrant parents what it meant to be an American. When each in turn became a naturalized citizen, they were proud as proud could be. They had finally arrived. They were finally accepted. They were a part of the greatest nation on earth and they were grateful for every step it had taken them to get there, to be together and to have a child born and raised on American soil.

During the war we kept our ears glued to the radio for news. I believe that my father even kept a shortwave radio at his business so he could find out if the Allied attacks on Germany were in the areas where his brothers and sisters were living. We also kept up on the news by reading *The New York Times* and *Life* magazine, which came out every week.

The conversation at the dinner table was always on current events or recent history. I had daily lessons from my mother and father on the events leading up to the war, the countries that were invaded, where the Allied forces were, where the Nazis were. During and after the war, my mother and father taught me about the Treaty of Versailles, which had established the shaky peace after World War I and made World War II all but inevitable.

My parents rooted for General Patton, and they saw right through the conniving of Stalin and Roosevelt. They were heartbroken when Roosevelt agreed to hand over the peoples and nations of Eastern Europe based on Stalin's argument that they were Slavs and ethnically tied to the Russian people. My parents believed that millions would suffer under Stalin's retribution and as long as Communism and Communist dictators dominated those nations.

During the war years, our parents or the Morrises used to take Jane and me to Saturday afternoon matinees at the Strand or Carlton theaters, the only two in town. The newsreels of the war shown before the movies were lengthy and vivid. It was another way that the hardships of the war were brought home to us.

At the theater I remember watching Walt Disney films. One that made a very strong impression on me was *Bambi*. I sobbed through the scenes where Bambi's mother was shot, while Jane, seated next to me, never shed a tear.

Whenever I was sick, my mother would let me lie in bed in the guest room, which was a little larger than my room and had a double bed. The bed would be covered with dolls, games and toys. Each day that I was sick, she would catch Stevie Morris coming home from school in the afternoon and send him to the corner store to get me a large vanilla and chocolate Dixie cup.

When the treaties ending the war were signed in 1945, I was sick in bed with a cold but it was a warm September day and the windows were open. I could hear celebrations in the streets, horns blowing. People were making merry, getting drunk and letting all the stops out.

When the war was over, *Life* magazine published gruesome photos of those who had been asphyxiated in the gas chambers. The horror of the holocaust as it unfolded in *Life* and the lesson it taught me on the nature of absolute evil incarnate in the Nazi high command has never diminished from my mind. Nor should it diminish from anyone's mind, lest we forget and such evil overtake us again.

In this regard I am grateful that my parents were realists and taught me to be a realist. They did not shield me from current events but made them a part of my life. Had I been deprived of this vital scene as it was happening, as we were living it, I would have been deprived of major elements of the preparation for my mission. The seed planted was unfolding.

When we were in the sixth grade, we were responsible for bringing a news story to the classroom. We had to be able to discuss it and explain it to the class. Sometimes the night before and sometimes the morning before I left for school, I would sit down with my mother to review the news so I could report on it. It was a difficult assignment. Current events were hard to understand without a background in recent history, but I worked diligently at it. I thank my mother and my sixth-grade teacher for seeing to it that we persevered in these assignments. I'm certain it contributed to my decision to major in political science and international relations in college.

8

Family

SIX MONTHS AFTER the war was over, in the spring of 1946, Mother received an urgent message from her family. Grandmother had a terminal illness and was not expected to live more than a few weeks. I was seven at the time. With little understanding of death or the deep ties that existed between my mother and her mother, and between my mother and her brothers, sisters, nieces and nephews, I could scarcely comprehend the gravity of the situation.

Through whatever connections my parents had, my mother was able to book passage for the two of us on one of the first nonmilitary flights from New York to London. Our passport pictures were taken, all the documents were in place, and the day came when I was to take my first plane ride. We were going to cross the Atlantic Ocean. It was the most exciting thing that had ever happened to me in my entire life! We said good-bye to my father and Barry, boarded the plane at LaGuardia Airport in New York, and embarked on a journey that was to expand my world awareness from the white picket fence of my play yard to international boundaries.

Mother had told me much about her childhood in Bulle and the pranks that she and her brothers and sisters would play. I had seen snapshots of my relatives, and on the calendars that regularly hung in our kitchen I had seen images of picturesque towns and villages, the countryside and the Swiss Alps. But it was impossible for me to imagine what it was really like in Switzerland. All the newsreels, radio and magazine coverage, all I had heard about around the kitchen table, and all the letters from Germany and Switzerland that got through during and after the war—all of this was nowhere near equal to the experience of being there.

It was a long flight in those days, on a propeller-driven plane. Throughout the trip, my mother was in mortal fear, while I was jumping up and down with delight. I told her not to worry, that God would see that we arrived safely, but she was not to be comforted. Finally, we landed in London and took a taxi to our hotel.

The sights of the bombed-out city told a story of horror. I saw what war had done and could do to a nation. Mother and I walked up and down the streets, and the scenes are as vivid to me now as they were when I was there. I will never forget them as long as I live. My soul knew what my mind was yet incapable of computing. But this I resolved: I had to live my life and serve my nation and other nations so that something as dreadful as this war could never happen again. I asked God to show me how I could prepare for my mission, to show me what my mission was and how he might use me to bring about world peace.

Within two days we crossed the English Channel by boat and then took a train to Geneva, Lausanne and our final destination at Territêt. Along the way we saw the wreckage and ravages of war. Not until we crossed the border into

Switzerland did we leave the war-torn countryside.

At Territêt we stayed at the home of Uncle Werner, my mother's younger brother, and Tante Marie. It was here that my grandmother was lying in bed suffering in her final illness. Uncle Werner and Tante Marie had two sons. The older was a teenager, named Dödi. The younger was Jean-Gustave, and he and I became fast buddies.

While my mother visited with her mother, Jean-Gustave and I played all over the apartment, in the courtyard and in the picturesque places of Territêt, which is on the shore of Lake Geneva. In the morning and the afternoon, we were allowed to visit our grandmother briefly. I was awed by her presence. I had never seen anyone on a death bed. The family prayed at her bedside and I prayed with them. She could not speak to me nor I to her, for I didn't know French and she didn't know English. But our souls communed, and a part of her became a part of me, a part that I have treasured all of my life.

Finally the day came when my grandmother was near her passing. The whole family gathered around her, including the children. Death was something that was a part of life, they said, and we should not be excluded from the event. And so it came to pass that at the age of seven, I saw my maternal grandmother draw her last breath. It seemed to me that there was little difference between life and death—being in the body or out of the body. As the soul gently made her final exit, I wondered if Jesus and his angels had come to take her in that moment. I could not see him or the angels, but I felt a peaceful presence of comfort and a sense that God was taking care of her. Death was a mystery but not unnatural. It was the logical conclusion of a life lived for the Lord, for her family and for her husband.

Not until years later did I learn that she, like Fridy, had dealt with a husband's alcoholism. My maternal grandfather was not living in 1946, so what I know of him are the stories of his jolly nature and how he used to play with his seven children.

Immediately following Grandmother's passing, the family convened at Uttewil, where a service was held. I remember watching as they lowered the casket into the grave and covered it over, and I remember placing a large wreath from our family on her grave. Relatives from all over Switzerland convened for the funeral, and so it was here that I met many whom I had not yet seen.

After the funeral we stayed in Uttewil and I got to know cousins and uncles and aunts who had remained there and were running the farm. We visited the homes of my mother's other brothers and sisters and their families as well as the brothers and sisters of my grandmother in the Schnyder family.

Each household and each family was quite different, the Enkerlis being the less well-off branch of the family, the others being well-to-do. And so I learned how people in various levels of society lived, worked, played, sang and danced. I established close ties with many of my cousins. Each one of them was dear to me and I admired their manners, their education and everything about their way of life. We also visited historic places, returned to my grandmother's hometown and went on hikes in the mountains.

9

Three Signs

BEFORE I WAS born and when I was very young, some seeds were planted that would spur me on in my ardent search for the masters of the Far East. In particular, three events occurred in my mother's life that enabled me to find out about these beloved masters.

World War I broke out while my mother was growing up in Bulle, Switzerland, and throughout the war Swiss soldiers were quartered in private homes there. A soldier was assigned to the Enkerli family, and my mother was responsible for keeping his room clean. On his nightstand she found *The Secret Doctrine,* by Madame Helena P. Blavatsky. She read it avidly, and this work inspired by the masters Morya and Kuthumi laid the foundation for her lifelong belief system. She acknowledged the existence of the masters of the Far East, and she accepted the law of karma and reincarnation as the only plausible explanation for the inequities of life.

The second event occurred while my mother was pregnant with me. Mrs. Weber, for whom she had worked as a governess in New York, gave her *The "I AM" Discourses,* by

Godfré Ray King. She told my mother, "Guard this book, for it is not for the profane. Keep it in your private library."

My mother told me later, "One night I fell asleep reading about the Mighty I AM Presence.* After some time I was awakened by a presence in the room. I saw a great light at the foot of my bed and said out loud, 'That's the Mighty I AM Presence!' and promptly went back to sleep."

My mother told me about a third contact with a higher power that occurred before my birth. The Oeschkers (the couple my parents had stayed with when they were first married) had given my mother the Christian Science textbook by Mary Baker Eddy, *Science and Health with Key to the Scriptures,* and the companion volume to it, the King James Version of the Bible. They also introduced her to a devout Christian Scientist who was to become a lifelong friend of my parents. Her name was Eva Schofield, and she was also a comforter and teacher to me throughout my early years. She lived in the country just outside of Red Bank. In later years she became a Sunday school teacher at the First Church of Christ Scientist, Red Bank, as well as a practitioner of Christian Science.

My mother used to tell the story of Mrs. Schofield's assistance when I was a baby:

> Betty Clare was less than a year old when she developed a severe earache. Nothing would stop her crying. I was so upset that I called Mrs. Schofield and held my baby to the phone after telling her what was the matter. I then took the phone to my ear to listen to what she had to say. She simply said "All is well,

---

* The *Mighty I AM Presence* is how Godfré described the Presence of God that is individualized for every soul.

Zellie,* all is well." Immediately Betty Clare stopped crying, all signs of her earache gone.

At that moment my mother knew that God had healed me through this devout woman, who applied the principles of Christian Science healing to my case.

After I had moved away from home and found the masters of the Far East, I discovered that I had been hearing their teachings when I was three years old. While my father was being held at Ellis Island, the ladies who came to take care of me during my mother's absences would read to me from *The "I AM" Discourses.*

Thus the seeds were planted of the three activities sponsored by the ascended masters that were to have a great influence on my life—Theosophy, the "I AM" Activity and Christian Science. But even though my mother believed in and accepted the principles of all three, she did not apply them actively or urge me to apply them. However, she did share her belief in reincarnation, which made perfect sense to me and which I confirmed in my own heart. And when I came upon the teachings of these activities (in the reverse order in which she had found them), she affirmed them to be true and gave me my freedom to pursue them.

---

* "Zellie," a Swiss nickname, short for "mademoiselle."

10

A Past Life

WHEN I WAS about four, suspended in that carefree realm of timeless, spaceless dimension that the child yet lives in, I was alone one day playing in my sandbox. The clouds were tracing forms of formlessness on the skyey canvas, shaping and reshaping themselves in fairy-tale motifs. The rays of the sun on the morning dew made the lawn and lilacs, the hyacinth, jonquils and forsythia sparkle like a crystal paradise in some far-off land.

I was secure in the definitions of the little white picket fence, caressed by the breezes and the soft flapping of the leaves on the giant silver maple as they showed their silvery undersides. My dolls were all lined up on the little painted wicker chair from Mexico. They were receiving a lesson on how to make mud pies for Daddy.

Then, gradually, gently, the scene began to change. At a certain point it was as though someone had turned the dial on a radio and I was locked into another frequency.

I was who I was, calmly centered in my heart. My soul was free, as free as the child I was. Yet I was not in Red Bank,

New Jersey, nor in the time frame of the present. I was idly playing on the sands of the River Nile, basking in the sunshine, comforted by the warmth of the sun and a mother's love. Playing there was altogether natural to me because I was secure in my native universe, secure in the God who was everywhere, the God whose flame burned within my heart.

As I sat there playing in the sand, I knew I was in Egypt. I knew I was on the Nile River. Then, as easily as my soul had glided into that scene, it glided back, and I was once again in my sandbox in Red Bank, New Jersey. The dial had been turned back to the previous station. Not even dazed, I jumped up and ran to find my mother. She was cooking at the kitchen stove. "Mother! Mother! What happened to me?" Then I told her step by step the story of what I had just experienced.

She sat me on a chair and sat down opposite me. With kindness and a certain respectful regard that my mother always had for me no matter what my age, she said calmly, "You have remembered a past life." And then, in words I could understand, she explained, "We have all lived before. We are sent here with a purpose and a plan. But it takes many lifetimes to finish the work we must do. Our body is a coat we wear. And when it wears out, we get another."

"Do we get a new mommy and daddy too?" I asked.

"Yes, we get a new daddy and we come back in another mommy's tummy. The soul is born once but it gets a new coat when it needs one. And when we come back again, the storybook of our life continues with the next chapter."

My mother then explained why she believed we had all lived before and would live again. "People are born different from each other," she said. "One child is born rich, another poor. One is good at many things, another is good at none. Good luck, bad luck. One is a genius, another can hardly learn to read and write."

"Why?" I asked.

"Because when we do good in one life, that good returns to us in a future life. When we are naughty and do bad things, that returns to us also. If you harm someone in one lifetime, you may be harmed in the next. This is how God's justice works, Betty Clare. Unless you understand that you have lived before, you will never understand why certain things happen in your life, both the good and the bad. If you practice the piano and study your lessons and you get good at it, you can bring it back in your next life. After several lifetimes of studying the piano, you could be born a child virtuoso like Mozart."

Still in the state of just having experienced a past modality, parallel to my present one, my child mind could easily grasp the reality that lay just beneath the surface of conscious awareness. My past life was a reality, and I knew what my mother was talking about. The concepts of reincarnation and karma were dimly familiar, embedded in the memory of my soul. I just had to be reminded because I was wearing a new body and I couldn't recall what I had known in other times and spheres.

I went back to my sandbox, content that life would unfold itself to me, that life would teach me whatever I needed to know in order to finish what I had begun as a little child playing on the Nile River. But the boundaries of my existence had been permanently altered. I now had a fixed coordinate somewhere in the distant past. I had relived a record of a past life. And that record, I felt certain, was one key to my destiny. I would never forget the experience.

Yes, I did think in these terms as a child. For after all, we *are* mature and ancient ones, even when we are children, inhabiting a child's mind and body. And the part of us that is timeless understands beyond the present. Such flashbacks may not be uncommon among children. But because there is not a wise parent or teacher to interpret the déjà vu, the child will often lose those early soul experiences beneath the shifting sands of the subconscious mind. Without religious training and a sense of the Self beyond the self, the soul may become the slave of the concrete, rational mind that screens out intuition and extrasensory perceptions that come from beyond the mental belt.

11

Searching for God

I WAS TWO years old when I had first met Jane Petherbridge, who was also two. Jane, her parents and two older brothers, Bill and David, had just moved in a few houses down on South Street. For Jane and me, it was like love at first sight. From that moment we were inseparable.

We played in my play yard and playhouse and in our garden. We wheeled our dolls in our doll carriages up and down the street. We rode our trikes and scooters, made sandcastles at the beach, chased the waves going out and ran ahead of the waves coming in. We jumped in sprinklers in the summer and made snowmen in the winter. On Halloween we went trick-or-treating, all dressed up in the costumes our mothers made or bought, carved our pumpkins, baked our cookies, split our raisins fifty-fifty. We had our agreements and disagreements.

At her house we ate Boston baked beans and brown bread, coleslaw and hot dogs. We built skyscrapers at my house with the blocks my father made, dressed up in her mother's clothes and shoes at hers, and laid out an elaborate plot to cover ourselves with sheets and scare our parents in the middle of the night.

Jane and I went to kindergarten together and were bosom buddies through the third grade. But that summer, two momentous events took place in our lives. One of them would tear us from each other permanently.

First, we began to notice that Jane's mother cried a lot and her father was seldom home. By and by the news came that her parents would be divorced and her mother had made plans to move back to Maine with the three children to live with Jane's grandfather. Jane and I were devastated at the thought that we could ever be separated.

The other momentous event involving Jane proved to be a key to my spiritual search. Before Jane's family moved away, her mother was trying to deal with the grief from the breakup of her marriage. Mrs. Petherbridge, who had come from a staunch Methodist background, was invited to attend services at the Christian Science church in Red Bank. Jane was going and I asked if I could come along. We were placed in Sunday school while her mother went to church. For me that day ended a long search.

AT THE AGE of four, I had begun looking for someone who could teach me about God. I pressed my mother to take me to Sunday school or to someone who could teach me. She said, "Betty Clare, you will have to wait till you are five." I think the year between four and five was the longest year of my life.

Finally she said, "Now I'm going to take you to Sunday school." I jumped up and down for joy. Happily seated in Sunday school at the Methodist church, I waited to hear the teachings of Jesus. But instead they made us color rabbits and

Easter eggs in coloring books. I kept waiting for the lesson but it didn't come. Then it came time for the collection and I put my money in the plate. Afterwards I asked the teacher, "What do you do with the money?" She said, "We give it to God."

I knew very well that God didn't need the money and that he didn't come and take the collection from the plate. I was hurt because the teacher had lied to me. When I went home and asked my mother what they did with the money, she said they used it to keep up the church, to pay the man who mowed the lawns and to pay the pastor a salary so he could support his family. This made perfectly good sense and I was satisfied, but I asked my mother to take me to other churches, not only to the Sunday school but to the adult services. I wanted to hear what the ministers were saying. I wanted to attend a candlelight service on Christmas Eve. I wanted to study under a Sunday school teacher who could answer my questions about God and Jesus and the Bible.

My mother took me to almost every Protestant church in town or asked the neighbors to take me when they were going. But each time I came away feeling empty, knowing that the message I was seeking was not there. Yet I still didn't know what that message was.

After those early excursions to the various Sunday schools and worship services, neither of my parents ever accompanied me to church, nor did they go themselves to a church of their choice, with a few notable exceptions. One of these was my father's attendance at Christmas Eve midnight Mass at Saint James Church. The other was the Easter sunrise service held at Atlantic Highlands, one of the highest points on the Eastern Seaboard.

I looked forward to that Easter service each year. My father and I would leave early in the morning while it was still dark, make the half-hour drive and be there when the service started before dawn. It was held outdoors and I was never dressed quite warmly enough for the chill of the morning air.

There was a minister, a choir and an organ. As the sun rose directly east, out of the Atlantic Ocean, the organist would play "Christ the Lord Is Risen Today." I thrilled to the sound of the Alleluias and felt a deep communion with Jesus. Each Easter I would reaffirm my commitment to him of all my life, all I could offer in his service. I felt my soul's tie to his heart. Jesus, the light of my life, the sun of my soul. "O Jesus," I would pray, "you saved me and my precious mother on Holy Saturday. Now use me to your purposes, O Lord."

We couldn't coax my mother to come along. I could never understand why. She had attended Catholic schools in Bulle, though brought up by Protestant parents.

My father was a confirmed Lutheran. He showed his faith by abundant works and the creed of the working man. Meanwhile, he retained his ties to that church, whose founder had proclaimed that salvation could be attained by faith alone without works.

For all his bluster and the blasts of hell that came through him when he was under the influence of alcohol, yet my father feared God. Many a night I would hear him crying out to God to help him. But my mother never prayed nor taught me to pray. She never spoke of Jesus or the saints. And to my loss, she never placed a single religious statue or painting in the house—no classical religious art, no portrait of Jesus or the Blessed Virgin or the Child Jesus.

The one exception was a terra-cotta plaque five inches in diameter that had a little angel in bas-relief painted white on a Wedgwood-blue background. My mother hung it over my bed, and it was there until I graduated from high school. It was the last thing I looked at before I fell asleep at night. It always made me smile. "Maybe," I thought, "there's a real angel peeping through that smiling cherub."

To my dismay, my mother also strongly objected to the Ave Marias played on TV or radio, saying they were overdone. And yet, with perfect gladness, she would respond to my requests to visit Saint James Catholic Church each time we went to town. She carefully instructed me in the proper mode of reverence according to Catholic traditions. She showed me how to kneel before the Blessed Virgin and to light a candle to pray for the sick or the deceased. Since that early training, I have always felt at home in Catholic churches around the world and have made pilgrimages to many shrines and cathedrals in Europe, the United States, and Central and South America.

Another exception to my mother's nonattendance at church took place on the occasions of the passing of her mother, sister and brother. After each of these events, she would go to a spiritualist church and take me with her, seeking a message from the beyond from her loved ones.

I was quite amazed as a child that a spiritualist medium or a minister could bring forth messages from the dead. My mother seemed pleased and comforted by the messages she received, while my eyes widened in disbelief. I was glad when she didn't take me to any more of those services. I didn't understand why we needed to hear from relatives who were in heaven. Perhaps through spiritualism my mother thought to reassure herself that if she could hear from her family members, she too would have a place on the other side.

What was most alarming to me about my mother's religious life, or rather the absence of it, was her fear of death. She was of strong Swiss stock and lived to be ninety-one, but she feared her oncoming death for thirty years before her passing. When she confided this to me in her later years, I reminded her that death was not real. I said that we merely shed the outworn coat we are wearing and the soul moves on to a new schoolroom of life (as she had once explained to me) or to one of the Father's many mansions where Jesus has prepared a place for us. I prayed with her and for her, but when the hour of her death came, her fear was no less.

AT THE AGE of six, seven and eight, I would ask Jesus to explain to me what the ministers were saying, and he would tell me the meaning of the parables. He told me that the ministers did not have the keys to the mysteries of God and of his kingdom, for his teachings had either been left out of the scriptures or had not come down to us as he had originally taught them. He said that in this age these lost teachings had to be restored and I would have a part in their restoration.

I was awestruck. How would I prepare myself? Where should I begin? I knew I must study the Bible. I yearned for a teacher who would lead me into all truth.

On that first day in Christian Science Sunday school, the day that I went with Jane, my prayer for a teacher was answered. I was convinced I had found the place that had the most advanced teaching on Jesus' message that there was to be found in my hometown.

After Sunday school I bounded in the door and ran to find my mother. I exclaimed, "Mother, do you know what I learned today? I learned the scientific statement of being by Mary Baker Eddy." Mr. Willard was my Sunday school teacher and he had loaned me a copy of *Science and Health*. Here is what I read to her:

There is no life, truth, intelligence, nor substance in matter. All is infinite Mind and its infinite manifestation, for God is All-in-all. Spirit is immortal Truth; matter is mortal error. Spirit is the real and eternal; matter is the unreal and temporal. Spirit is God, and man is His image and likeness. Therefore man is not material; he is spiritual.[7]

"Mother, this is what I've always believed! I have finally found the right Sunday school."

I had always known that matter was not real, that what we see is not the permanent reality we have come from. I had always known that God's mind is universal intelligence and that mind is everywhere, because everywhere I went and whatever I was doing, I was in contact with that mind of God. I knew that everything around me was in a state of decay and disintegration—the flowers, the trees, the grass, the animals, the people. We see material life and death but we don't see the spiritual life beyond. I am made in the image and likeness of God and I had always known it, and now somebody was telling me what I had always known.

My mother nodded her agreement with everything I said. She had long since become accustomed to my religious inquiries. I said, "Mother, have you ever heard of Christian Science? Have you ever read this book?"

Mother looked at me as though she was about to make a confession. The moment of truth had come. Then she said, "I not only have a copy of Mrs. Eddy's book, but I also have the Bible that goes along with it." With that she proceeded to tell me the story of God healing my earache through Eva Schofield and that she had received the books from Mrs. Oeschker.

My mouth dropped open with the realization that in all of my searching since the ages of four and five, my mother had not told me about the Christian Science church. She had never introduced me to the practitioner who had befriended her in her hour of crisis, nor to the books that had been placed in her hands—if not for her own learning, then indeed for mine.

MY LOVE FOR Jesus was great, and I came to love Mary Baker Eddy as my dearest friend. She gave me my awareness of the absolute reality of God-good and the absolute unreality of all that is the antithesis of that God-good. I loved attending the Sunday service and wished it was not held at the same time as Sunday school so that I could go to both.

I loved the Wednesday night services too—the scriptural readings, the testimonies, the people, who had such an expression of understanding in their eyes, an expression that I hadn't found anywhere else in my searchings. At last I met people who could answer my questions about God and Jesus and what Jesus taught and how we could apply that teaching today.

I also met Mrs. Schofield, who became my spiritual mother. My own dear mother would gladly drive me to her home so that she could talk to me and I to her. I would come away from those meetings with my cup filled with light, my joy knowing no bounds, as though I had touched the hem of Reality.

My spiritual convictions were strengthened. The roots of my spiritual dependence upon God grew deeper. The windows of heaven were opened to me. And I could weather the storms that broke around me. Jesus Christ was the Rock of Truth and the open door to my Father-Mother God.

My contact with Mary Baker Eddy, who, much later I learned, had been embodied as Mary of Bethany, also quickened my own sense of having been among the disciples in Bethany two thousand years ago. My mission was unfolding, though all the pieces to the puzzle were by no means in place.

From that day on I was a Christian Scientist, and I stayed with the Christian Science movement until the age of twenty-two, when I met Mark Prophet.

Jane Petherbridge and I attended Sunday school together through that summer in 1948. Then moving day came at the Petherbridge house. We watched as all their furniture and household items and clothes were packed. The vans pulled out the next morning. Mother and I saw Mrs. Petherbridge, Bill, David and Jane off on the train to their new home in Halowell, Maine. I sobbed uncontrollably. Life would not be the same.

Not until the first day of class in the tenth grade, when I met Geraldine Scalone, did I have such a close friend again. Geraldine was a beautiful and loyal friend. We spent many good times together in those growing-up years and left Red Bank High and Red Bank with no regrets. We both knew that our lives were headed for major change. And though we went our separate ways, we met again in Santa Barbara many years later.

FINDING THE CHRISTIAN Science Sunday school was not the end of my search. Though I read *Science and Health* and other writings by Mary Baker Eddy every spare moment, I was eager to experience the religious life of my classmates.

One time some Jewish friends took me to a Friday night service at the synagogue in Red Bank. I wanted to understand the religious service of the Jews, for had not Jesus come out of the Jewish tradition? And had he not preached in the synagogues? When we arrived, there was a general look of consternation and then a hush. Then one mother asked in a friendly voice, "Betty Clare, what are you doing here this evening?" I answered simply, "Oh, I'm just visiting."

The service was in Hebrew, so of course I didn't understand it. But I would have liked to, because I had such a great love for the patriarchs and prophets of the Old Testament. I would have liked to have gone to Hebrew School and studied what the other children were studying, but it was not to be.

In fourth grade I met Norma Jean Ivins. She lived with her parents, older brother Louis and grandmother a few long blocks away. A shortcut through my backyard and the connecting driveways of a few more houses brought me to her door in no time. Sometimes I would just ride my bike the long way around with Barry following at a good doggie clip.

The Ivins were Seventh-Day Adventists. So through them I was introduced to the church founded by Mrs. Ellen Gould White. We drove some distance out of town to get to the church, and for me it was an adventure. I enjoyed the sermons, the hymns, the Sunday school and the people, and I gained a background in the Bible and its literal interpretation from Genesis through Revelation. When Grandmother Ivins told me that one day fifty-pound hailstones would fall upon the earth, my eyes grew as wide as saucers. Grandma Ivins taught me a lot about the Bible. There wasn't a time I was in their home that I wasn't learning something about God.

The Ivins were vegetarians, so I was introduced to soybean and gluten products that were meat substitutes. I loved saying grace before we ate, and I loved the food and wanted my mother to prepare meals the way the Ivins did. But my parents were not about to be converted to vegetarianism, nor to saying grace.

When I stayed overnight at Norma Jean's, her mother would read to us from the Bible or from Seventh-Day Adventist Bible stories for children. Before we went to sleep, Mrs. Ivins, Norma Jean and I knelt beside the bed. I was thrilled to see how other people prayed to Jesus and to God and how a Christian home was kept by devout disciples of the Lord.

I also took note of their belief that the Sabbath should be kept on Saturday, in the tradition of Jewish law. From sundown Friday to sundown Saturday, activities were dedicated to the Lord. Happily for me, I could attend the Seventh-Day Adventist church on Saturday and the Christian Science church on Sunday.

One day I came home from church with the Ivins and I announced to my mother that I wanted to become a Seventh-Day Adventist. She said, "I am glad that you are in the company of such nice people and that you have enjoyed their services. You may continue to attend church with them and to study the Bible with them, but you must wait until you are twenty-one to decide what church you will become a member of." That was the end of that subject.

By the time I was twenty-one, I no longer wanted to become a Seventh-Day Adventist. But the comfort I derived from fellowship with these humble souls, as well as their example, will always be with me. Their love for God and Jesus was reflected in their conversation, in everything they did and in their sweetness to me. And I learned how other families lived their lives in peace in the Lord—such a contrast to my own house.

12

Earning My Way

MARIA MONTESSORI TEACHES that children in their teen-age years have a deep need for independence. And one of the things that spells independence for them is economic independence. If you can't go out and earn enough money to feed and clothe yourself, you feel insecure and a certain amount of anxiety. This was true for me when I was young, so I found all kinds of ways to make money. In fact, I started long before I was a teenager.

Around the age of seven or eight, I realized that it was my mommy and daddy who gave me Christmas presents. I would hang up my stocking and my stocking would be filled, but nobody gave them Christmas presents. I wanted them to be able to hang up their stockings and have them filled and for them to have presents too. So I figured out how I was going to do this.

In the summer I would go into the forest to pick violets and bring them home. I would arrange them nicely, put them in tinfoil and then go door to door selling them. Sometimes I would do this with Norma Jean Ivins, and her mother (the

Seventh-Day Adventist) would kneel with us and lead us in prayer for our mission. The dog and cat who went with us also had to kneel in prayer, putting their little paws together. We would say a prayer to Jesus to bless our wares and let us find those who needed what we had to offer.

I remember the great leaping of the flame in my heart when I would come with my violets and ring the doorbell. People would be so gracious, and they would receive me and talk to me about my violets. They would give me a quarter for a bunch. I remember the experience of the Holy Spirit in that interchange. It was a ritual of interaction with angels and elementals, and a distribution of joy.

There were also people who would greet me at the door and say, "What are you doing knocking on my door and bothering me?" or "Who are you, you little kid, coming up to my house with your violets?" I would walk away with my head hanging, and then I would go and pray and ask God to help me so that people would receive me. It was good training for my mission.

ALL SUMMER LONG and through the fall I saved my pennies and quarters and fifty-cent pieces. I would go downtown to the five-and-ten and I would look for something pretty. I would buy a little vase or perhaps curlers or hairpins for my mother, or socks or handkerchiefs for my father. I would hide these gifts in the closet until I had enough to fill my mother's stocking and my father's stocking and enough presents to put under the tree. It took me six months to do this.

Christmas came and my mother would open her presents. But my father refused to take his presents out of his stocking or to open them. I would beg him, "Please, Daddy, open your presents." The day after Christmas I would beg him, "Please, Daddy, open your presents." He would gruffly refuse. Ten or fifteen days later, after the Christmas celebration was all over, he would finally feel so guilty that he would reluctantly open his presents. The next summer it would start all over again, and this went on year after year.

My father never bought me a present. If there were presents under the tree, my mother had bought them with the money she earned from babysitting. My father bought nothing for me, and he was not about to receive anything from me. He spent his money on his liquor and his cigarettes and whatever else he spent it on.

WHEN WE WERE eight, nine and ten, Norma Jean and I would go to the men's sock factory on Newman Springs Road and bring home bundles of looper clips. This word isn't in the dictionary, but it's what we called the clipping from the top of the sock which formed a loop. We dyed them crimson, blue, green and yellow and made potholders to sell. One time I sewed a dozen potholders together to make a bathmat. We also made pincushions out of beautiful silk remnants from a tie factory and sold them door-to-door.

Our mothers showed us how to open a savings account, and we would carefully deposit our money in the bank. Looking back on that experience, I see that it was important for me to make my own money, to save my own money and to be able to spend my own money. I remember earning a small amount of money for a large amount of work when I used to do babysitting, which included scrubbing floors, housekeeping and many other things.

When I was sixteen, I was paid something like a dollar an

hour to scrape barnacles off the bottom of a boat—scraping and scraping those barnacles for hours on end. After an hour, that dollar was a lot of money to me, and I wasn't going to spend it on frivolous things. It meant a lot because I worked hard for it.

13

The Demons of Alcohol

ACCORDING TO TODAY'S thinking, I would be called an adult child of an alcoholic. But in those days, I didn't know that my father would be considered an alcoholic. It never would have occurred to me. I thought an alcoholic was somebody who drank all the time and was drunk all the time. But I did know that my father had a serious drinking problem and was often inebriated in the evenings. In retrospect, I was an "adult child" from the day I was born.

In time it became clear to me that it was his drinking problem that made him engage in the verbal abuse of my mother. He had a violent temper, and when he yelled he could be heard by neighbors on all sides, much to my mortification. Although his anger was almost never directed against me, I took personally the insults he hurled at my mother. This went on all of our lives, but I was less aware of it as a child, perhaps because I spent so much time in the home of my Greek neighbors.

My father was a great guy when he was sober, but that was in the morning, at noontime and in the afternoon. Most nights were a nightmare, unless he came home early to work in the garden or we worked on projects together around the house.

Except for those occasions, I didn't see much of my father in the hours of his sobriety, because he got up early to go to work at his boatyard. When he was sober, I found an intelligent, reasoning, kind and concerned parent, someone it was fun to be around. Later in the day, though, his other self, the drunken self, would emerge. Then he was a composite of himself and his deep levels of anger, along with whatever demons were unleashed through that anger. When he had had just a few drinks, he was so emotionally unstable that he easily took offense when no offense was intended.

Daddy was five foot ten or five foot eleven and never weighed more than 140 pounds. He was wiry and all muscle. He had blond hair, brown eyes and deep lines on his face. Strikingly handsome in his youth, he was a ladies' man all his life. In earlier years he wore a white shirt with a black tie, khaki pants, his white captain's hat and a pea jacket. The outfit never varied. It was his uniform, and everyone called him "Cap" or "Cap'n Wulf."

Although he was a genius at building yachts that were admired the world around, my father was not a businessman. After the war he was burdened by a combination of postwar depression, poor business sense, undercapitalization and a lack of advertising dollars. But his drinking was the overriding cause of his downfall. A steady stream of cash was going down the drain as he entertained prospective buyers (always a drinking crowd) at the local yacht clubs or at the Silver Bar, just up the alley from his office. His routine was beer and a jigger of Scotch (for him a volatile combination), and another, and another.

By the early 1950s, he couldn't hold on to his business and was forced to sell out to his competitors. After that, he repaired boats. He wore the same khaki pants and pea jacket with the same black tie, but now it was a khaki shirt, instead of a white shirt, and khaki captain's cap—perhaps a symbol of his self-demotion.

As I watched him over the years, I came to realize that little by little the alcohol was destroying his reasoning faculties—his ability to think clearly and logically and to make decisions. I saw a man, a husband, a father, a mother, a marriage and a home destroyed by alcohol.

It broke my heart, but not all at once. For as I witnessed this for eighteen years, something inside of me died a little each day. The hopelessness that things would never change, the expectations that would never be realized, the promises that would never be kept.

But I also bear witness that something was reborn in me each day—the hope, the faith, the charity of Jesus Christ. The lesson brought home to me each day was that I must put my trust in God, not man. Then one day as I pondered the dependable goodness of God and the undependable goodness of man, I realized that again God was teaching me the First Commandment. And he expected me to understand it and obey it: "Thou shalt have no other gods before me."[8]

This meant that I must not make an idol, good or bad, of my parents, myself or anyone else. I must recognize the good in all people as God's and the evil as a misguided expression of free will. I must exalt the good in everyone and shun the evil. And Jesus' words rang true: "No man can serve two masters: for either he will hate the one, and love the other; or else he will hold to the one, and despise the other. Ye cannot serve God and mammon."[9]

THE ONLY THING certain about an alcoholic is the uncertainty. I never knew what state Daddy would be in when he came home. But I could tell by the way the car sounded in the driveway whether he was in control.

If he had already had one too many, he would hit the bumps harder and the old Buick would bounce a bit before coming to a stop just in front of the garage doors that he had embellished with leaded glass windows. His footsteps on the back steps and the way the door slammed would tell the rest. This would happen anytime between five o'clock and nine o'clock. I never knew, but I was tensed for the moment whenever it would come.

He would hang up his pea jacket and captain's hat on the hook in the hall and sit down at the head of the kitchen table. Mother always had a meal ready by five o'clock, and she would heat it up whenever he got home. Daddy ate like a bird, so with or without food, he had little to cushion the effects of the alcohol.

Each evening I would sit at the table, in between Father at the head and Mother opposite him, near the stove. Across from me, where my toy chest used to be, Daddy had put in a large picture window so we could see the lawn and garden while we ate. I had the best view. Daddy had built an intricate Bavarian birdhouse and feeding station that we could pull up to the back steps to replenish with scraps and to clean. Red geraniums grew in window boxes. A cuckoo clock and souvenirs of Germany and Switzerland hung on the wall. It was a homey atmosphere.

He had also installed in front of the window a wooden stand for five large tropical fish tanks and one smaller tank—two forty-gallon tanks on the bottom shelf, two on the top shelf with the smaller one in between, and a fifth large tank on another low shelf next to it. Raising tropical fish of every kind had become a hobby Daddy and I shared. The plants in the tanks grew luxuriously because he planted them in a layer of fertile soil on the bottom of each tank and then added a thick layer of gravel on top. Friends and acquaintances would come from miles around to admire his garden and his tropical fish, just as they admired his boats and his skill in remodeling the house.

He needed praise and appreciation, so Mother gave it constantly and told me to do the same. She told me he had built a house for his parents in Elmshorn on one of his trips home from Venezuela and his father had never acknowledged it or thanked him. She excused his behavior on the basis that he had had a hard life with his stern Prussian father. I have wondered if he was also an adult child of an alcoholic.

Often my mother would beg my father not to have another drink before dinner. He would ignore her, and the beer and schnapps would take its toll before my eyes. I never said a word, but sat in pale silence eating my food. Steadily the Daddy I loved would recede, and sentimentality and melancholy would take over. This preceded the foul language, the cursing, the condemning of Mommy for not being a good wife. Much of the fuss centered around the food not being right—a combination of my father's taste buds being desensitized by alcohol and the meal sitting on the stove for hours.

One particular night when I was twelve or thirteen stands out in my memory. It started out as a night like all other nights. The meal ended in unpleasantness, yelling and accusations. Then my father left, slamming that old kitchen door as he did every night, until one day one of the boards finally split in two. He went to the library and sat down in his red leather chair, where he would usually fall asleep watching TV. It was over for that night. Or so we thought.

Meanwhile, Mother and I were lingering at the table with small talk. All at once Daddy came to the door to yell at us another round because "the two of you are talking about me behind my back." Mother protested that we had not been talking about him at all (which was true), but he would have none of it. In a moment's pause, his mind changed gears. Then a wild, purposed look overtook him. Calmly, deliberately, he walked to one of the large fish tanks and kicked it. The glass shattered and forty gallons of water rushed out, fish and all, as he calmly, deliberately walked out.

Instantly I was galvanized. I grabbed every available pot, pan, bucket and pail. I had to save the precious fish that were now flopping all over the kitchen floor. Mother and I worked as a team. As soon as I had a bucket of fish, I ran outside in the dark fifteen or twenty yards to our goldfish pond, dumped them in, ran back to the kitchen, gathered more fish, ran back down, dumped them in. This was repeated four or five times till I could find no more fish. Then the mop-up began—forty gallons of water plus dirt and gravel. How long this took I don't know. I was in a time warp—stunned by the violence, frantic to save the fish.

When it was over, my mother and I collapsed into our chairs in silent shock. My father's energy (or the negative force that used him) was so intense that it suppressed any feelings we might have had. No more than five minutes had passed when he burst through the kitchen door again. It was a replay. Calmly, deliberately, crazed, he walked to the next tank and, "O my God!" he kicked it in. The glass shattered and again forty gallons of water rushed out, fish and all. Calmly, deliberately, he walked out. It was sheer madness.

We moved into action. Mother and I scooped up all the fish we could find into a pail of water, and I ran down to the goldfish pond, dumped them in, came back, scooped up, ran down, dumped them in, et cetera, et cetera. Then we mopped up. Again we fell into our chairs. Numb.

A third time the door opened. Now I was watching the scene in slow motion. My mind could not believe what I was seeing. My father walked over to the third tank as if programmed, kicked it in and walked out. The three-ring circus was on. By this time we knew our act. Our performance was flawless. And this time it was really over.

Daddy sauntered off to bed, weaving his way up the steep staircase, and the time-space warp we had been in closed. It was so unreal, as though it had never happened. But it did.

The morning after the fish-tank ordeal, I didn't see Daddy. Mother said he had no recall of what he had done. His prize collection of rare fish and plants was gone, much to his sorrow. But he never apologized for the torment he had put us through. We just picked up from where we had been. I went to school, he to work and Mother resumed her household duties.

14

Home Life

IN MY EARLIER years I had nowhere to run to, nowhere to hide. I knew I was here to stay until God should deliver me of my assignment at 43 South Street. But the day I learned to ride my bike I had a new freedom. I rode all over town and out into the country. My bike riding gave me the space I needed to think things through and put some distance between me and the troublesome situation at home. I had to figure out who I was apart from my parents' world.

I was not the object of my father's outbursts. They were always directed at my pitiful mother, who would plead, "Hans, please stop." But he never did. Neither he nor the demons of alcohol respected her. And as a silent witness, I was also a victim. His invectives grazed me as they whizzed by. His anger knocked me out emotionally. I would black out a half dozen times during a nightly ordeal. Once his tirade started, nobody would move in any direction, including Barry, lest his passions be fueled.

One summer's night when I was in another part of the house as it started, I slipped away and rode my bike a few miles toward Fair Haven to be at peace and contemplate what life would be like in a "normal" home.

But what was normal? I had no standard by which to measure normalcy. Next door, Mr. Morris never yelled at all. He was like a sweet Greek Buddha. Mrs. Morris would get excited and go after one or more of the five children in a flurry of Greek that would send them running to do what they were supposed to be doing. But in her I never felt the intensity of anger that I did from my father at those mealtime scenes. And the Morrises didn't drink.

When Daddy would take me to the Silver Bar or to the yacht club and order a coke for me, everybody would be drinking. If we stayed too long, they would get louder and louder and happier and happier, until the sentimental singing and the melancholy set in. And that could be followed by somebody getting nasty or insulting and somebody else having to be escorted or carried out. I had witnessed my father being driven home (and me with him) by more sober buddies who refused to let him drive.

When I went babysitting and the couple came home late, the husband, who would drive me home, had often had a few too many. When driving with these husbands or my father, I made it a habit of affirming "God is driving this car" as they sped around curves and ran lights. The scenes repeated again and again.

On that bike ride, the one and only time I absented myself from the nightly scene, I saw that there was nowhere else for me to be but home, such as it was, until God should choose to lift me out of it and put me somewhere else. It was my duty to be there. He had put me there for a reason, and I would not leave my father or my mother until I had fulfilled my reason for being there. Maybe by being there I could bring some lightness, some happiness to their hearts.

So I rode back home as it was getting dark and resumed my part in this play and interplay of light and darkness. Was it a melodrama? Was it a tragedy? Was it a comedy of errors? I didn't know. Because I was a player caught in the middle of each act.

But this I did know. I had to be responsible. When they were not in control of themselves or circumstances, I had to be in control. For who else could be? I must keep the trust.

I TURNED TO God, to Jesus, to the Bible and *Science and Health* and to the beauties of God in nature, where I always found peace and strength. From prayer and the affirmation of Truth and the laws of God underpinning every hour of the day, I drew upon a reservoir of light and joy that never failed me. It was the wellspring from on high. The Comforter was with me.

From dear Mrs. Schofield and dear Sunday school teachers such as Mr. Willard, Mrs. Gorsuch and Mr. Ernest Ruh, as well as the weekly Lesson-Sermon that I read and studied as often as I could, I learned to apply impersonal principles of God's laws to personal day-to-day problems. At the Wednesday night healing services, I heard testimonies of Christian Science healing. I believed in God's healing power and I prayed that he would make me an instrument of that power when I grew up.

Much of my comfort came from the hymns written by Mary Baker Eddy. I loved to sing them and play them on the piano. I loved them all, but one comes to mind:

Shepherd, show me how to go
O'er the hillside steep,
How to gather, how to sow,—
How to feed Thy sheep;
I will listen for Thy voice,
Lest my footsteps stray;
I will follow and rejoice
All the rugged way.[10]

IN THE MIDST of seeking and truly finding God, I saw my mother's spirit broken day by day, a little at a time. My mother had a great deal of fear all of her life. Her fear of my father was all-consuming. As a result, her life revolved around him.

Twenty years before she passed on, she confided in me that she was afraid to die. I could hardly believe that the one who had told me of reincarnation and the continuity of the soul feared her own death. I told her she had nothing to be afraid of, but she truly needed Jesus and Saint Michael the Archangel, as we all do, to take her across the astral sea.[11] I urged her to pray to them and go to the church of her choice, since Christian Science was not for her. It was then that I realized that without God in the center of her life, she was also afraid to live. And without God, she surely did not have the power to challenge the force that preyed upon her through her husband.

The house was dominated by my mother's fear and my father's impending anger. I never knew when or for what unimaginable reason the next explosion would take place, or the next, or the next. Their anger and fear were in polarity, aggressive and passive—and always there just beneath the surface, waiting to be ignited.

They never considered marriage counseling. And as for therapy, it was unheard of. They were stuck in their own response mechanisms to each other, as the same scenes played themselves out day after day, year after year.

The saddest part of all was that neither parent had a real and living relationship with God or Jesus Christ. They seemed more fatalistic and superstitious than truly spiritual. I saw this when Daddy taught me the law of karma as he had gleaned it from his own life. Cigarette in hand and in a sober, passive mood, he would say, "Betty Clare, it all comes back to you. It all comes back to you." Instead of seeing this law of the circle as opportunity for resolution, regeneration and resurrection, he viewed it pessimistically, almost like a doctrine of final ends wherein God's judgment, not his mercy, was the only out.

Where is mercy? Forgive us our debts *as we* forgive our debtors. As Hans did not extend mercy to Fridy, would God extend mercy to him? As Fridy did not extend mercy to Hans, would God forgive her?

I don't know. Because God has free will—the same free will he gave to his sons and daughters with the first photon of light and the first breath of life. He may choose to bind himself by his law or to bend it. But he will not break it. For he is both Law and Lawgiver. "Even so, Lord God Almighty, true and righteous are thy judgments," true and righteous are thy judgments.[12]

My father was not necessarily humbled by his discovery of God's law. I had seen him defy that law as the gods defy the Fates. When his doctor told him that if he didn't stop smoking he would die in three years, he said to me, with that look in his eye that made me shudder: "Like h— I'll stop smoking.

Over my dead body!" And three years later, on winter solstice 1984, he died, smoking and drinking to the end. How sad. How sad. And the river of tears that never flowed from my eyes at the kitchen table now flowed—not for me and not for him, but for the many he had injured with his fury, and principally my dear mother.

WHAT TAKES OVER the mind in the night side under the influence of alcohol? After observing Hans Wulf for eighteen years, there is no doubt in my mind that possessing demons take over the mind and emotions when the blood alcohol content creates its chemical imbalance in the body. And I believe that my father was tormented by these demons as much as my mother and I were.

Is an alcoholic responsible for what he does under the influence of alcohol? Indeed he is. He is responsible for taking the first drink. Can he help himself? Only if he is willing to say die to the demons who "made me do it" and to ask God for help when he cannot help himself. Until that day, the karma for broken lives and broken spirits keeps piling up.

My mother would be called a "codependent," the term applied to someone who passively accommodates the aggressive behavior of the alcoholic. Is the codependent, in this case the wife, responsible for the actions of the alcoholic? She is responsible for not seeking professional help for herself and her husband and for not just plain refusing to tolerate the state of affairs any longer, including the victimizing of the child. In this situation there are demons of fear, a traumatizing fear, that paralyze all bystanders caught in the net of the demons of alcohol. There is no excuse for any adult to stand by while an alcoholic engages in the nightly assault of the soul of a child or anyone.

What is lost in such cases is the child's right to be a child, and the baby's right to be a baby. The adult child of an alcoholic has to go in search of the baby he or she was not allowed to be, the child that never was a child. To retrieve the lost parts of the self may take years or a lifetime or longer.

Instead of confronting my father directly when he was sober, my mother dealt with his tirades by talking it out on the telephone with her friend Agnes Schwenker the morning after. She spoke disparagingly of him to me, gossiped about him, and instructed me about how I should behave in order to appease him and avoid conflict.

The balance to all of the problems brought on by my father's alcoholism was the work ethic. Our family worked hard and often worked together on remodeling or painting the house. I was my father's helper, and I learned a lot about carpentry, painting, plumbing, wallpapering and exterior remodeling. When we put a knotty pine recreation room and bar in the basement, I stripped the bark from the wood and had a part in each phase of the job. My parents held an open house when it was all finished and lots of people came to see it.

Together we tended the garden, gathered fruits and berries to make jams and jellies, canned produce, and preserved the harvest of our garden for winter. My father was a good cook (he had actually taught my mother how to cook), so once in a while we prepared meals together. My father was so diligent in his duty to do a day's work that his very work habits set a pattern of stability within an unstable situation.

I delighted in working on the yard, mowing the lawn, raking the leaves and shoveling snow as well as in keeping the house clean. I learned how to clean house almost professionally from Angie and Elvira Morris. Once a week I would go through the house from top to bottom—dust-mopping, washing floors, vacuuming, dusting and polishing furniture and periodically cleaning the windows inside and out. Since I was an only child and my mother didn't like housekeeping, these chores fell to me and I was happy to do them.

My respect for and devotion to my parents was absolute. Whatever they asked me to do, I obeyed. I honored them no matter what, and I loved both of them dearly. When Christmas or their birthdays approached, I made them presents or bought them gifts with pennies, nickels, dimes and quarters I had earned in selling my handmade pot holders or violets I had picked in the nearby woods.

During the storms of my parents' relationship, I always remained silent, even though I couldn't separate myself from them. I could not cry, but my heart cried. My father's anger suppressed all other emotion my mother or I could express. I think that a part of my child self was depressed and unexpressed most of the time, even while another part was in communion with God. Long after the tirade was over, we would sit in silence, then slowly begin to pick up the broken china, bring order to the kitchen, perhaps finish our meal, do the dishes and go on living—I to my homework or, in later years, to babysitting jobs; mother to her sewing or knitting.

THE PROBLEMS AT home were reflected at school in my relationships with other children. I didn't have role models to teach me what was normal or abnormal in a social situation. Because I perceived myself as being responsible for my father and mother and for their problems, I carried this sense of responsibility to my classroom.

Jane had similar burdens to bear. At an early age she had to grapple with her own mother's problems with her father and the divorce that followed. We both saw her mother cry often, and she told us why. So we were both responsible "little women." And as the smartest kids in the class, we also became our teacher's pets, which didn't help matters with our classmates.

My grammar school teachers said I was mature, responsible, bright, serious. These qualities in me reflected both their presence and their absence in my home life. My parents were serious in shouldering the responsibilities of their home and business and of rearing me. They were intelligent and hard-working and had a rich heritage of being self-made, seeing the world and mixing with all strata of society. They had an international consciousness, were broad-minded, and made me aware of what was going on in the world in my earliest years.

But when it came to the problems between them, neither one seemed capable or desirous of changing. They seemed totally preoccupied with their karmic relationship. And any sensitivity they might have had to the pain their arguments were placing upon me was not enough to cause them to change.

In many areas of their lives, my parents demonstrated the law that life is problem solving, that life is suffering, and that when we have problems and when we suffer, we summon our forces, use our ingenuity and solve those problems. My father and mother were both creative and inventive. If there was a job to do, they figured out the best way to do it. They would assess a situation, figure out what was possible and what was not possible, what was within their means and what wasn't, come up with viable alternatives, select the best and make it happen. What they never quite figured out was their relationship to God, to Jesus Christ or their spiritual path.

My father's violent temper and drinking problem was a non-subject, except for my mother's pleadings, which were powerless to bring about change. My parents would fight openly in front of me. Each would speak to me disparagingly of the other in his or her absence. My mother was by far the worst at this. She also spent hours on the phone telling friends and neighbors about my father. She would condemn him behind his back and at the same time praise him to his face and to friends and neighbors when she was proud of his accomplishments. She feared and respected him and was tied to him in a love-hate relationship that my child mind could not comprehend.

She made me a party to business burdens, financial burdens and my father's affairs with other women. It was as though the roles of parent and child were switched. She put me in the position of being her parent, her teacher, her confidante. I had the world on my shoulders. And the idea that my seemingly poor saintly mother had to endure all that she did for my sake did not escape me.

From birth to age eighteen, I witnessed the almost daily clashes between my father and mother. It seemed endless. I could speak of these goings-on to no one. I was ashamed of my father. I wondered if the neighbors on either side of us could hear his yelling, and I was always embarrassed to walk out of the house in case they had. I was ashamed of my mother, too, for not dealing with the problem by directly confronting it.

It just went on and on, year in, year out—my father's anger, my mother's fear. Yet, she was the one who so often quoted to me the words of Franklin D. Roosevelt that had galvanized a nation: "The only thing we have to fear is fear itself."

Since I saw myself as the cause of all of their problems (much later, I learned that this is the psychological posture of most children of alcoholics), I thought that there would never be a resolution until I graduated from high school and permanently left home. I looked forward to the day when I would go out to make my way in the world, thereby liberating both myself and my parents. Then we could make decisions that none of us could make while we were together under one roof at 43 South Street.

15

Friends

IN JUNE OF 1952, Mother took me to Maine to visit Jane Petherbridge and her family. We rode the Greyhound from Red Bank to Augusta, Maine, and it was unbearably hot on the bus. But the reunion with Jane was joyous. It was refreshing to meet her friends, school chums and church acquaintances. We renewed our ties, though we had never stopped writing.

My mother's great joy in going on this trip with me was twofold. She was able to get away from my father for a while and from washing dishes and looking after him. And she also wanted to show me the historic sites from Red Bank to Augusta.

I had never been out of the area where I lived except to go to Switzerland when I was seven and one year when I went to the Catskills. So taking a trip to New England was like discovering the world. I was totally enthralled by it all.

For me the highlight of the trip was touring Boston. We went to the state capitol, with its golden dome, Faneuil Hall and the historical sites of Boston. My mother was a history buff, so I got a taste of the history from her and from the guides on the tours. We also took a bus to Marblehead and went to the Wayside Inn, which Longfellow had frequented, and saw the Longfellow house in Cambridge.

Since I was already a student of Christian Science, we visited the Mother Church, which also had a large dome, and the Christian Science Publishing Society. At the *Christian Science Monitor,* we saw how newspapers were made. And we visited the first little church that Mary Baker Eddy built, then a larger church she built later.

Through her writings and the hymns she wrote, which I played in Sunday school, I had learned to love Mary Baker Eddy. Now I was seeing what she had done, the fruit of her life. After she built the first two churches, she started printing the *Christian Science Journal* and the *Christian Science Sentinel.* Then she gave her board of directors the order to found an international daily newspaper, and the publishing society was born.

I had been attending Sunday school in the garage of a little house in Red Bank. It was a thrill for me to realize that I had a connection to this big church and this imposing building. It made me feel I was a part of something that went beyond Red Bank.

I had a vision of this church and its teaching going around the world. My vision was that Mary Baker Eddy's books and teachings would be everywhere in the world and that I had some role to play in making this happen.

THE NEXT SUMMER, I visited Jane again, this time without my mother, and spent the summer with her in Maine. We had great times at a cabin on a lake, went swimming and toured

Augusta, the state capital. The next summer Jane came to Red Bank for a month and we spent part of our vacation on Long Beach Island. My father was building a marina and beach club near Beach Haven, at the southernmost tip of the island.

Jane's family became involved in the Methodist church in Halowell. It was there she would meet her husband, Clifton Ives, a Methodist minister's son who followed in his father's footsteps. I attended their wedding, a most happy occasion. In later years, I shared with her some of the spiritual teachings I had found. But Cliff, though he was a nice guy, could not accept them. And I accepted that her life fully revolved around him and their church work together.

Like Jane, I also married a minister and went the way of my husband's calling. In a sense, then, our lives ran on parallel paths, both of us choosing to minister to those who need spiritual guidance and love and a deeper understanding of the path of our Lord. I am grateful to God for this friendship and for all it has meant to me over the years, truly the joy of my childhood. What a beautiful thing it is for children to establish lifelong ties that outlast mundane events. My heart is sure that this soul tie will endure beyond this life, even as it preexisted it.

I remember a card Jane sent me during the long years of our friendship. It was a quote from Shakespeare: "But if the while I think on thee, dear friend, all losses are restored and sorrows end."[13] My sentiments are the same.

JANE AND I had been solid buddies while she was in Red Bank. But even then there was a clique of girls in grammar school who tried to pry us apart, to get at either one of us. When Jane left, I was fair game. It must have been some karma from a previous life that these girls moved against me every chance they got.

One of the things that burdened my relationship with these girls had to do with birthday parties. Somewhere around fourth or fifth grade, my mother said to me, "I cannot afford to buy gifts for these girls through the year when their parties come up. So I'm not going to allow you to attend these birthday parties." When the next party came along, I declined. People thought I just missed it because I was ill or something. Then I declined the next one, and the next one. I remember some of the girls saying, "Well, if you're not going to come to our parties, we're not going to come to yours." After that I never had another birthday party again, and I felt like a social outcast as a result of it.

One of the most painful situations I remember happened around seventh grade. A group of girls were forming a club, and we were meeting at the apartment of one of the girls. All the other girls said they wanted to blackball a particular girl. They got me in a room and pounded on me and said, "You have to blackball her. You have to do this. She shouldn't be in this club." I kept on protesting and saying, "She has done nothing wrong. Why should she be blackballed?"

In the end I gave in to their pressure and said, "OK. We'll blackball her." As soon as I gave in, everybody turned on me and said, "Because you voted to blackball her, we're blackballing you and you're kicked out of the club." The whole group kicked me out, and I walked home alone, in a lot of pain. I couldn't in any way articulate my grief. I was just silent. I couldn't tell my friends about my problems at home and I couldn't tell my father and mother about my problems at school. This group of girls continued their cruel jokes and silent scorn throughout grammar school and high school.

THERE WAS ANOTHER group of kids who were a year ahead of me in school. They were intelligent, college bound, and I liked them a lot. I had known some of them since childhood. At one point in high school, they wrote me a letter and said that they had seen how the kids in my own class had treated me and they wanted to invite me to be a part of their group.

One of the boys from that group invited me to go to a dance. I went with him, and other kids from this group went to the dance too, and I had the time of my life there. However, subsequent to that, I didn't take them up on their invitation to be a part of their crowd. There was some kind of pall over me, or a weight. I was burdened by my household situation. I was burdened by the girls in my school excluding me from their social events and their particular clique. It seemed that if I couldn't be in that clique, I felt totally defeated.

These other kids who were a year ahead of me were a lot of fun. They would have been an inspiration to me for getting into college. Not accepting their invitation was one of the decisions in my life that I should not have made. I should have made the decision to join them and have fun with them, as I easily could have.

I would have been in their class in school, except that my mother had a choice to either put me in school with other four-year-olds or to put me in school a year later. She decided it was better for me to be at home with her another year. Although this was difficult for me, apparently she made the right decision, because I met the people of my karma. And for whatever I may have done to them in a past life, I call for forgiveness.

16

Blacking Out

WHEN I WAS in the third grade, I was in a Christmas play. We had rehearsed for many weeks. Our parents, teachers and the entire school were present. When it came time for me to say my lines, which I knew well, all of a sudden I blacked out. Five, ten, fifteen, twenty seconds passed, maybe more. I don't know because I wasn't there. It was as though someone had shut off the switch. I had no consciousness, no self-awareness.

Then just as easily, I was back again, as if someone had turned on the switch. By this time the play had gone on without me. I didn't understand what had happened. I couldn't explain it to my teachers, classmates or parents. Unbeknownst to me or them, this was the beginning of a life-long occurrence that would come upon me anytime, anywhere without warning.

Classmates made fun of me. Some teachers thought I was faking. One teacher in particular was determined to "shake the devil out" of me. As I would reenter this plane of awareness after "blacking out," I would find her holding me by my shoulders and shaking me as hard as she could, while the class looked on.

The boys nicknamed me "Spellbound," and my parents and I had to come to grips with a daily reality that mystified all of us. My mother took me to a doctor at the New York Medical Center. At that time they called my condition petit mal epilepsy. Today these are known as absence seizures. They gave me medication. I felt drugged and didn't feel normal when I took it, so within a week I told my parents I wasn't going to take it. No other medical attention was given to the matter.

WITHIN THE YEAR that these lapses began, I had a serious accident that came about as a result of one of them. Mother had sent me outside to hang up the sheets, towels and Daddy's pants and shirts on the clothesline to dry. Instead of finishing the job, I started playing with my dog, Barry. I used to run up and down the cellar doors that slanted against the house. They were the kind that opened in the middle and covered a stairway that led to a basement which was almost entirely underground. To "beautify" the house, my father had recently installed half-inch-thick glass portholes from one of his boats.

On that day when I ran up the cellar doors, I put my left leg through one of the portholes while holding Barry in my arms. I remember hearing the glass crack and my foot beginning to sink. The next thing I knew, I came out of a lapse in consciousness to find that my leg had fallen through almost to the crotch and I had pulled it out. Thus, I was badly cut in both directions. My entire left leg was covered with blood. In the middle of all of this Barry had jumped from my arms. I went to look for a neighbor or my mother to help me.

Instead of applying pressure to stop the bleeding or calling an ambulance, my mother called my father, who was out on the river. He finally sent one of his workmen, who drove up in what looked like a Model-T Ford. They sat me in it and drove me to Riverview Hospital. When I finally got to the emergency room, I heard the doctors saying to one another, "We may have to amputate her leg." I calmly spoke to them and said, "God is going to heal my leg." As they were sewing me up—some sixty stitches all told—they repeated this prediction a number of times, "We may have to amputate her leg." Each time they said it, I replied, "God is going to heal my leg."

Mother was annoyed at me, and when my father finally arrived, he was upset. The last thing I heard the doctors say to my parents was, "Her leg may never grow." Again I affirmed, "God will heal my leg." After I was released from the hospital, my father took me home and laid me on a cot in the living room. When we got home, I asked my mother to call Mrs. Schofield, the Christian Science practitioner who had silenced my cries as a baby with her, "All is well, Zellie, all is well." She prayed for me, as did many others of various faiths. I am grateful for their love.

Classmates came to visit me and brought me books to read, and I was pretty much stationary for the rest of the summer. I can remember thinking to myself, "God must be punishing me because I wasn't obedient to my mother. I didn't hang up the clothes on the clothesline when she told me to."

I remained convinced that something I had done had caused me to have that accident. I couldn't believe that God would give me such a punishment for disobeying my mother, but I couldn't think of anything else I had done to warrant that accident. I loved God and I knew that he was a merciful

God and that whatever my sins were, he was making me pay for them. But in the process he also forgave me, and by his forgiveness I believed that my leg would be fully healed to serve me in my life's mission—whatever that mission was to be, for I didn't yet know what it was to be.

For a couple of months my mother and I walked to the doctor's office to have my bandages changed. I can remember how painful it was when he would tear off the adhesive tape. By the end of the summer my leg was healing nicely and I was allowed to go in the ocean, even though the wounds had not fully healed.

Not only did God heal my leg completely and see to it that it perfectly matched the other leg, but he has given me the strength to stand at the altar of God and on the lecture platform for five and six hours at a time. Many years after the injury, as I toured the United States, South America, Europe, Australia, the Philippines, I often wondered what I would do without my legs. And I think back upon that accident that could have been worse but for the grace and mercy of God.

ON ANOTHER OCCASION I again had a chance to see the miraculous salvation of our God. I was riding my bicycle in heavy traffic one summer day. (Don't ask me why my parents thought I could ride a bike all over town with the problem I had.) Streams of cars were converging from Monmouth County Racetrack, Fort Monmouth, and the seaside resort crowd. I was pedaling toward a five-street intersection when once again I blacked out.

By this time, a number of years after my leg injury, I had disciplined my inner being to be in control of my body during these lapses of consciousness. In this case, I continued to pedal my bike, but I was pedaling harder than usual. I was suddenly brought back to bodily awareness by the impact of the front wheel against a steel overhang on a drain gutter. The force of the impact threw me and my bike quite a distance into the air. I landed with a considerable bounce, but without falling off the bike. As I looked around and assessed the situation, I saw drivers on all five streets hanging out of their windows looking at me. I realized they had been anticipating a serious accident, but I was protected and survived unharmed. I shall never forget the gratitude I felt for this divine intercession.

Later in life, when I was introduced to Saint Michael the Archangel as the angel of protection and faith, I realized that it was he who had saved my life on that day and seen to it that no harm had come to my body. I testify that in looking back, I see the presence of Archangel Michael with me all the years of this life and many lifetimes. Surely without the grace of God implemented by the angelic hosts, I would not have been able to accomplish what I did in my life.

AS I RECALL the incident of my leg, I realize that it must have been a karma from a past life. At the time my soul truly knew that this was a returning karma I must bear and that divine justice must be satisfied, even as divine mercy does intercede to save us from ourselves. I also understand that this and other karmas I faced as a child were given to me to "clear the decks," so when I came to my mission I would have already balanced certain karmas that would have prevented me from fulfilling all I have been able to do in my years of service. I also realize that my soul had asked for my karma to descend at birth so that I might more quickly balance it prior to the time when I would be called to work for God.

I do not regret any part of my life or any circumstance, any setback or any challenge, especially those I faced in childhood. I am profoundly grateful for the gift of Christian Science and for Mary Baker Eddy, whom I always felt to be a personal friend on the road of life. I have looked philosophically upon my lot and have attempted to extract from each situation morsels of truth and a deeper understanding of life's mysteries. I have sent my questions to God as I cast them into the universal sea of light. And by and by—sometimes immediately, sometimes in a matter of days or even decades—God has sent back to me the answers to my questions.

I believe in divine justice and that there is no injustice anywhere in the universe. Although human justice is more often a miscarriage of divine justice, yet I know, I believe and I affirm that ultimately all things come to us for a reason. If we learn our lessons well from each situation and encounter, we will not have to repeat them.

I believe that earth is a schoolroom and we are here to study and apply a practical life teaching. We are intended to graduate from this schoolroom and to move on to the next, whatever is most suited to our level of development.

17

The Trials God Gives Us

I CAN TRUTHFULLY say that I have never railed against the Almighty when life seemed hard. But I have cried out to God to help me, to help me bear the burdens that I now understand to have been the burdens of my karma.

But not all trials are karma. Some of our trials are for our strengthening and for testing the mettle of our souls. God has to bear down upon us a little bit and then a little bit more to see whether we are willing to bear the burden of the Lord.

And what is the burden of the Lord? I was to learn that it is both his burden of light, even the Christ-truth that is despised and rejected of men, as well as the burden of world karma. Although world karma may not be our own, as we are strengthened in the Lord we desire to bear some portion, small or great, of that karma. Thereby others who are not strong enough to bear it might know surcease from their pain and suffering because we have chosen to bear our own karma, and then some. As I often tell my students, God has a right to test us and we have a right to be tested—and to pass our tests.

In addition, the challenges along life's way are a series of hurdles given to us because our souls have desired to be initiated. When we are on the path of soul evolution and we come to the point where we desire not only to love the Lord our God with all of our soul and mind and heart[14] but to *know* the Lord our God with all of our soul and mind and heart, then the Lord sends a master to teach us, to train us and to purge us of all ego-centered human habits and conditionings. And this is so that we might become "sacred bread for God's sacred feast," as Kahlil Gibran phrased it.[15]

Thus, all who seek God must know that life's circumstances must be seen as karmic possibilities, both positive and negative. They are the testing of our souls, that both God and we might know our strengths and our weaknesses as well as our spiritual, mental, emotional and physical fitness to fight the good fight and win. Each day, each cycle is a round of initiation. With each initiation passed, we gain greater self-mastery and eventually the restoration of our original birthright as sons and daughters of God.

Dealing with records and momentums of karma and seeking divine as well as human resolution with every part of life brings soul freedom and opportunity to seek, find and fulfill our divine plan. Accepting trial and tribulation cheerfully, gratefully and energetically with a can-do spirit has its rewards in soul satisfaction. God cares enough for us to test us so that we may have a sense of co-measurement with him. It is written that "whom the Lord loveth he chasteneth, and scourgeth every son whom he receiveth."[16] We are his beloved, and he loves us enough to try us in the fires of his love, for only thus can we enter the kingdom of God.

If, then, beyond soul testing, we desire a path of initiation wherein we engage in the battle of light and darkness and deal directly with the forces of Christ and Antichrist, we will know persecutions and ultimately the crucifixion. Of this path Jesus spoke when he said, "There is no man that hath left house, or brethren, or sisters, or father, or mother, or wife, or children, or lands, for my sake, and the gospel's, but he shall receive an hundredfold now in this time, houses, and brethren, and sisters, and mothers, and children, and lands, with persecutions; and in the world to come eternal life."[17]

Ultimately, this is the path of personal Christhood taught and demonstrated by the saints and adepts of East and West throughout the ages. Those who embrace it enter in to the joy of their Lord and ultimately the initiation of empowerment. Jesus spoke of this initiation when he said, "All power is given unto me in heaven and in earth."[18]

AS A CHILD, I had the sense of the path of Christ the burden-bearer. I did not understand all of the above, but I sensed that God was working out some grand and noble purpose in my life. And though I did not understand all things, this one thing I did understand: God was indeed requiring my soul to "bear all things, believe all things, hope all things and endure all things."[19] For so the apostle Paul taught me in his sermon on spiritual gifts.[20] Without that mighty love, that self-givingness called charity that bears, believes, hopes and endures all things, none of the gifts of the Spirit are valid.

My faith and my hope in God were the foundations whereby I ultimately received, through the Sacred Heart of Jesus, the gift of charity and of Christ's unspeakable love. Only when I received the full gift of charity through initiation could I look into the mirror of my soul and see there the reflection of Christ's love. Then I began to know the mysteries of Christ's love and then I began to know my soul as I am known, as the beloved of God. And by the conversion of Christ's love, I was born again, not by water or by blood, but by the Spirit, the Holy Spirit, of my Lord and Saviour Jesus Christ.

When I was a child, my heart desired to be obedient to my parents, to my teachers and, most importantly, to the voice of conscience. This voice of God within me became more articulate the more I would listen, trust and obey. When the voice of my inner counselor would counsel me, I would not only obey but I would reason with my Lord. For did not the Bible say, "Come now, and let us reason together, saith the LORD"?[21]

I would ask questions. I would seek to understand why things were happening to me, why things in the world that seemed so unjust and so cruel were happening. Sometimes the inner teacher would teach me, and sometimes he would be silent. And in the silence and the stillness of my meditation upon God, I would also learn of him and his laws.

By and by, I could distinguish between the voice of my inner teacher and the voice of my Jesus. And then I learned to know the voice of God—gentle yet mighty and always there—though sometimes I would have to clear the clouds that would come between me and the sun of God's presence, clouds of dark karma and disappointments that made me cry out, "How long, O Lord!"

Walking and talking with Jesus gave me great comfort. Within my mind the all-knowing presence of Jesus would affirm to me the truth or the error of the situation I was in or give me a profound explanation. I have been instructed in this way all my life, and this is how I have come to understand many things I know today. I didn't think that what I was doing was anything different than what anybody else could do. I thought everybody walked and talked with God.

WHEN I WAS a child, I was not yet perfected in the Law. But I believed that when that which is perfect, even Christ, would come into my temple, then that which was done in part would be done away with.[22] I was not perfect in obedience to my father, mother, teachers, to the voice of conscience, to Jesus or to God. But I was learning day by day that the price I had to pay for each act of disobedience was so great that it was simply not worth it to disobey God or those whom he had sent to me to teach me, to train me and to raise me up in the way that I should go.

I began to understand that in order to obey, I had to listen and to listen carefully, whether to the inner voice of authority or to the outer voice of authority in my life. In order to listen, I had to have a listening ear. I had to desire to hear the word of God and the word of my instructors. I could not turn a deaf ear to God or to those he had put in charge of me. I must hear God by the hearing of the inner and the outer ear. And as a little child, I simply must trust and obey.

Thus, in the same childlike trust and obedience that I was being trained in by my parents and in which I was training myself, I came to accept my blackouts as a gift of God, perhaps not ordained by him but at least allowed. And if they were allowed, they were indeed allowed for a purpose.

Certainly my inner will to surmount the problem was being shaped and shod with the strength of the Lord. But not until the age of forty did I have a clue about what might have caused it.

18

My Mother's Confession

ONE DAY WHEN I was visiting Red Bank, Mother and I were sitting alone at the kitchen table talking about the years gone by over a cup of coffee and some fresh-made apple pie. Suddenly she turned to me and said, "Betty Clare, I have a confession to make."

She looked down, almost ashamed, looked up and then down again. Then she said, "When I found out I was pregnant with you, I didn't want to have you. It wasn't personal of course. Daddy and I were married in 1937, the business was just getting started, and we didn't have a permanent home yet. I thought we should wait a little while, maybe a year or two. So I called a pharmacist and asked him if he could give me something to take to stop the pregnancy."

By now my heart was pounding. I couldn't believe what I was hearing.

"He said, 'Of course, Mrs. Wulf, I understand. Come on down to my pharmacy. I have just what you need.'" Then Mother looked up at me and said, "He gave me a drug and I took it."

There was a long silence as I looked at her in disbelief. And then I said, "Oh, great! Well, it didn't work. I'm here." The shock of my mother's rejection was upon me, then the gratitude that I had made it in spite of it all.

Now I realize that my mother thought that the drug she took may have caused my childhood blackouts. For nearly thirty years she had borne the guilt of her act and what she thought were the consequences. I had compassion for her because I could understand—given who and what she was, burdened as she had been all her life by fears and doubts— how she could have felt compelled to make such a decision.

I myself did not put two and two together until a dozen years later, when I decided to find out what kind of drug a pharmacist could have given a woman to abort a child in 1938. A gynecologist told me that it would have been quinine sulfate. And depending on the stage of pregnancy, which I assume must have been in the first trimester, it could have damaged the developing central nervous system and the brain. Thus, Mother's worst fears could have been well-founded.

In my growing-up years and throughout adulthood, I had felt a certain ceiling on my mental faculties and memory. I felt that if I could just get through that ceiling, I could access a compartment of my mind that had not been available to me since birth.

I am grateful to you, Mother, for having had the courage to reveal this to me so that I could pursue the healing of my psyche and my psychology as well as my physical body. Through fasting and prayer and with the Lord's help, I have worked on purging this drug and its effects, physical and nonphysical, from my body and mind. And I have experienced a liberation from many limitations I have felt all of my life.

However, throughout my life I have also been conscious

of the higher mental body, as the vessel of the mind of Christ, bypassing the limitations of mind and memory and establishing direct awareness of facts, figures and information as well as a direct knowledge of sublime realities. This awareness and this knowledge have not come to me through the rational mind but direct from the vast storehouse of the mind of God, as it can come to others who tap in to that vast source.

MANY YEARS AFTER these events in my life, the ascended master El Morya gave me some insight into them. He told me, "You were slated to be a vegetable from puberty on, but by your tremendous inner will you prevailed over incalculable odds. You took command of your physical brain and body and ruled them by your inner Being. You fought the good fight and you won." El Morya also stated that this attempted abortion was not my karma, nor was it intended as a soul testing, though indeed it came to be that. It was the crucifixion of my soul and my body in the womb.

One day, in deep meditation, I went back to the memory of my experience in utero when this drug was introduced into the developing fetus, which my soul was already occupying. It was indeed an agony on the cross. As I was in meditation, my legs began to shake uncontrollably; then my entire body began to quake. This continued for a full hour. As I allowed myself to re-experience the scene, I saw that prior to the introduction of the drug, my soul had been set for the mission. Afterwards I had to deal with the desire not to be, not to live, not to be born.

By the time my gestation in the womb reached full term, I was still struggling with the foreknowledge of what would be my lot if I was born in that body. This accounts for the delay and difficulty in my birth—Mother having been in the hospital in pain for two weeks, the doctor making the prediction that I would likely not survive.

Seeing all this and knowing that the true will of my being had been shrouded by a drug that had temporarily daunted my will, my beloved Guru, El Morya, cut across the dilemma and made a decision on my behalf that I was not able to make. In typical Morya style, he sent Dr. Rullman to deliver me by cesarean section.

My meditation on my experience of the drug concluded with the moment Dr. Rullman lifted me out of my mother's belly. Until that moment I had not wanted to be born, so much so that I was sobbing in my meditation-regression. Then I knew, then I saw. Looking up into my father's eyes, I saw not only my father, but beyond my father I saw my Guru.

Thus, I entered life with the understanding of so great a love—that of the living Guru who carried me across the abyss and placed me in my father's waiting arms. My Guru of many lifetimes knew that I would have wanted him to override my will in favor of God's will, no matter the price I would have to pay. Without El Morya's love and his moving upon my father and Dr. Rullman, my lesser, unenlightened will might have prevailed and I would not have been born in this life to fulfill my reason for being.

This is one reason that my love for El Morya is so deep, so unspeakable. The Guru-chela relationship under the sponsorship of an ascended master is the noblest friendship one can know. El Morya knows me better than I know myself. He acts in my best interest, knowing that I will catch up to the standard and the vision he holds for me and be where I need to be on time.

Thank you, Mother, for bearing with me to the end. I do

forgive you with all my heart. I am so grateful for all you have given me. And my adversity, though at times piercing my heart with a pain not of this world, has been tempered by God's grace. It has summoned from the depths and the heights of my being an indomitable will to be and to become all that I really am in God.

19

Sundays

SUNDAY WAS A special day in our house. Daddy was home and we three enjoyed a pleasant breakfast together. A delightful music program played on the radio each Sunday morning as we were eating breakfast. I was totally charmed by it. A beautiful orchestral rendition of Viennese waltzes was accompanied by the singing of untold numbers of canaries. As soon as the music started and the birds heard it, they would begin the most beautiful singing of the nature kingdom that I had ever heard. It became a part of our Sunday morning ritual.

While I was dressing for Sunday school, Mother was already preparing Sunday dinner. It might be roast beef with potatoes browning in the oven, string beans seasoned with parsley and a little bit of nutmeg, and often cauliflower with a cream sauce seasoned with pepper, Maggi and nutmeg.

Another Sunday dinner I looked forward to was fresh kale cooked overnight with pork and served with new potatoes, boiled, pealed and then rolled in uncooked cream of wheat and fried to a golden brown. This meal always had plenty of leftovers and the second and third time we ate it, the kale and potatoes were fried in the kale juice and the cut of pork went along with it.

Along with these hardy meals, Mother always served a salad I helped her prepare. Like all the other dishes, it was my father's recipe. Finely chopped white onions, Gulden's mustard, salt and pepper, apple cider vinegar and vegetable oil, lettuce from the garden, including Boston, red leaf and salad bowl, with fresh tomatoes was our summer salad, while bought iceberg, romaine and sometimes endive were the winter fare. Cut-up celery, celery leaves and parsley were optional. Daddy enjoyed an avocado before his salad and I got a little slice now and then.

My favorite dessert was "floating islands." Mother made a vanilla cream with egg yolk and thickening, topped with freshly beaten egg whites flavored with sugar and vanilla. Sometimes she would soak a little pound cake in wine and put it at the bottom of a large bowl from which she served the dessert.

Sunday dinner was the only meal we ate in the dining room. During the week the dining room table served as a sewing station, a desk where I did my homework, or a flat surface where my father spread out his big stamp collection, which he would work on night after night for a stretch, especially in winter. I also had a stamp collection and worked at it with him by the hour. As I studied the stamps, I became interested in the countries that issued them. I read *National Geographic* and other magazines to increase my understanding of what was happening in different countries and the world in which I lived.

After a big Sunday dinner, I looked forward to Sunday supper later on, which was often cooked fruit with pudding or pancakes. Mother made a delicious cornmeal pudding with raisins. She had a special aluminum pot, like a cake pan with a hole in the center except it was taller and smaller in diameter. It had a top that sealed and locked, and she cooked the pudding by immersing this pot in boiling water. Then she made a fruit sauce from whatever fruits were in season—blue plums, apples, berries, pears, et cetera. When the corn pudding came out, it was sliced and topped with the hot fruit sauce.

The same kind of sauce was served over German pancakes. These are made from a thin batter of eggs, flour, milk, water and salt. The size of a large dinner plate, they were fried in bacon fat and bacon bits in a black skillet and served two or three thick. Sometimes my father would make this meal since it was his recipe. He was a good cook and enjoyed cooking when he wasn't too tired from a day's work.

Another Sunday night supper was made with blue plums halved. A large rectangular cookie tin was lined with a pie crust and a single layer of blue plums, one against the other in rows. They were sprinkled with sugar and a little lemon juice and then baked. The pieces were cut about five inches square and put on our plates, all we could eat. Assorted German and Swiss cheeses were sometimes served on the side. It was simply delicious!

These were the '40s and the '50s before everything became processed, chemicalized, devitalized, sprayed and poisoned with insecticides. I ate the all-American diet, which in our family was based on a German diet. So I had plenty of pork, meat three times a day, bacon and bacon fat on my toast in the morning, eggs every day before school, every kind of beef dish, chicken, turkey, Swiss cheeses of all kinds, and always a tray of German sausages made fresh with the best meat by the local German butcher.

These were the "healthy" foods of our time. Our parents

thought they were giving us the best. Little did they know that with this kind of a diet they were sowing the seeds of heart problems, stroke, cancer and all of the fatal diseases that have come upon this generation.

SUNDAYS WERE SPECIAL to me for more than food and family togetherness, because it was the Lord's day and I looked forward to receiving understanding that always opened doors beyond doors into realms of light. Jesus had taught me that I could not live by bread alone but by every word that proceedeth out of the mouth of God. He also said, "He that loveth father or mother more than me is not worthy of me: and he that loveth son or daughter more than me is not worthy of me."[23] My perspective was clear on the matter.

After breakfast I got dressed for Sunday school. My mother made most of my clothes and I helped, so I learned to sew at a young age. My favorite Sunday dress was made of a beautiful Swiss fabric with royal blue, pale blue and white stripes. It was the truest blue I had ever had in a dress. The stripes came to a V in front, and the dress had a plain V-neck, simple sleeves and a gathered skirt. That dress lasted for years because my mother left extra length in the bodice so she could lengthen it from the waist as I grew. Every other Sunday I wore a dress of similar design that had alternating two-inch green and white stripes with tiny dark green roses sprinkled all over the stripes. I wore white socks with either white or black patent leather shoes, a little purse to match, a straw hat and white gloves.

The ritual of dressing up in my Sunday best made me feel ready to go to the altar to hear the words of Jesus as they were read from the Bible and as I heard him speaking to me in my heart. The keys to the scriptures which Mary Baker Eddy received from God answered so many of my questions. But still more were not answered. I trusted they would be answered in time, just as soon as I would be ready to receive them and God would want me to have them.

As I said good-bye to my parents and walked out the front door, I skipped down the brick steps and the slate sidewalk, turned left, crossed the street diagonally and, with Mrs. Ottinger's permission, walked through her driveway and through the gate in the chain-link fence that separated her backyard from the backyard of the house one street over on Hudson Avenue. Beyond that driveway I turned right, crossed the street diagonally and entered the back parking lot of the Christian Science church, which fronted on Broad Street, the main street in Red Bank.

Since neither of my parents ever attended the Christian Science church with me, I was accustomed to walking alone and communing with God. God was saying to me, "If you want me, you will have to come and find me."

This experience taught me to walk with God and to walk alone. And I learned that if I wanted something bad enough, I had to find the resources within myself to get it. If I wanted to go to Sunday school, I would have to go by myself, and I did. God was fashioning a bold and independent spirit. Strong-willed, I would not be moved from my course. And the seed of the mission was growing.

I can still remember the exact places here and there along the way to church where I received revelations from God or Jesus. I could go to those spots today and tell you what the Lord spoke in my heart. Some were mysteries of the kingdom that have remained sealed in my heart, and some I have revealed in my writings and sermons.

ONE VERY SPECIAL Sunday, as I walked to church reciting the Twenty-third Psalm, the gentle presence of my Lord overshadowed me. And I affirmed, because I *knew* it deep within my heart, "The LORD is my shepherd; and because he is my shepherd day and night, I shall not want. I shall not want." These words sealed my heart in the heart of Jesus. He carried my soul to green pastures, where I could rest and know regular intervals of return to the Source and enter the still waters of his mind. God was restoring my soul. He was leading me in paths of righteousness.

After that, when I was present for the almost nightly confrontations between my parents at the kitchen table, I could recite the words in my heart, "Yea, though I walk through the valley of the shadow of death, I will fear no evil: for thou art with me; thy rod (the rod of thy Law and thy Presence) and thy staff (the staff of self-knowledge and the knowledge of God) they comfort me."[24]

How true it was that God had prepared a table before me, in fact two tables. One was at home, in the presence of mine enemies—the elements of my own mortality that I must pluck out, the demons of anger that raged through my father, and the demons of fear that stalked through my mother.

The second table was a feast of light. I saw it with a pure white cloth and crystal vessels. It was a heavenly vision, with candles burning and the Lord present. If this was the table prepared for the saints in heaven when they should sup with him in glory, it was also the feast of truth of which I partook at Sunday school and in my quiet hours of reading the Bible and studying the works of Mary Baker Eddy. God was anointing my head with the oil of divine understanding, and the cup of my heart was running over with his love.

When I sought to commune with God, it was natural for

me to recite the Psalms. Immediately I was uplifted. I remember feeling light, God's light, come upon me in a shower of spiritual energy. God's gentle presence would enfold me, and I had the sense of a physical vibration around my head that was tangible.

Each time this would happen, I would hear a roaring sound in my inner ear, like the sound of an ocean wave or the roar of Niagara Falls. In that mode I would be listening to God with my inner ear in a heightened sensitivity. Simultaneously, I would be seeing with an inner vision.

As a child, it was altogether natural for me to feel God's light all around me. I was literally in the glory of the Lord, and my heart rejoiced in the gladness of knowing that all of his promises to my soul from the beginning would be fulfilled. I was at peace.

WHEN I FIRST started Sunday school, we met in a large two-story garage that had been nicely renovated for the Sunday school service and the classes that followed, which were separated by age group. The adult services were being held in the main house. By and by a beautiful colonial-style church edifice was built.

I would arrive at Sunday school with an expectant heart and a sense of wonder as to what God would have in store for me today. Sometimes the girls in my Sunday school class would giggle and disrupt the lesson. But every moment was so precious to me. I was receiving my soul nourishment for the week to come, and I knew only too well how much I needed it. I savored every morsel of truth that came out of the mouth of my teacher.

During the week I would study the Lesson-Sermon, which

consisted of selected passages from the Bible and *Science and Health* compiled by the Christian Science board of directors. The topics, which were derived from headings designated by Mary Baker Eddy, included such things as "Spirit," "Soul," "Mind," "Life," "Truth" or "Love," as well as arcane titles such as "Ancient and Modern Necromancy, *alias* Mesmerism and Hypnotism, Denounced." Christian Scientists study the Lesson-Sermon for the week and then hear it read on Sunday morning in church. In Sunday school we read parts of it aloud and discussed the meaning of the scriptures as well as Mary Baker Eddy's interpretation.

I used a system of steel dividers in my book and marked the verses with blue chalk that was easily erased. Each time I read the lesson or even one section of it, I would be immersed in light. Often verses of scripture would stand out as though highlighted in light. The words of the prophets, Christ Jesus and the apostles burned in my heart as a living message. The name of God "I AM THAT I AM" stood out in letters of fire as did Jesus' statement "I am the resurrection and the life"[25] and the statement by John that "God is love."[26]

I CAME TO Christian Science with a deeply personal love for Jesus, and through Christian Science this love was enriched. I felt that I contacted him as the person he was in Galilee and the Master he is today.

On Sunday afternoons at five o'clock, "The Greatest Story Ever Told" played on the radio. Each program was a segment in Jesus' life. I listened enraptured, as though Jesus were speaking to me directly and I was hearing him speak these words to me directly. These programs, together with the Seventh-Day Adventist Bible stories and my own reading of the scriptures, would not allow me to relate to Jesus only metaphysically. To me he was a very real being.

One of Mary Baker Eddy's hymns begins "Saw ye my Saviour? Heard ye the glad sound? Felt ye the power of the Word?"[27] But Christian Science does not articulate the Christian doctrine of being saved by Jesus Christ and being born again through the conversion of the Holy Spirit. Christian Science also does not teach that Jesus died for our sins. And it minimizes the importance of the crucifixion and maximizes the resurrection.

I myself could never understand the Christian doctrine that proclaimed that two thousand years ago Jesus died for my sins. The pastors and Sunday school teachers I encountered never could quite explain to me how Jesus' death two thousand years ago could atone for sins I had not committed at that time, sins of this life or those I might commit in the future.

Only when I received the ascended masters' teachings did I truly understand the concept of Christ dying for the sins of the world. I learned that Jesus was the Son of God whom the Father had sent to bear our karma for a time. I learned that God, through Jesus Christ, forgives our sins. But his forgiveness does not exempt us from paying the price for those sins—in other words, balancing the karma of the misuse of free will and the misqualification of God's light, energy and consciousness. Christ's forgiveness is the act of setting aside our sin, or karma, so that we can pay our debts to every part of life through service to our fellowman, devotion to God and a path of discipleship under Jesus Christ.

Jesus bears the sins of the world because the weight is so great that if we had to bear that weight, we could not simultaneously balance the karma for that sin. It's like getting out of debtors' prison so you can work to pay off your debts.

I also learned that the transfiguration, the crucifixion, the resurrection and the ascension are steps of spiritual initiation that one day every son and daughter of God must pass through. By these teachings from the ascended masters as well as the mysteries that Jesus has been revealing to me all of my life, I finally understood the erroneous doctrines that continue to be taught by Christianity today. And I achieved a resolution of my soul with the divine doctrine of Jesus Christ.

My understanding of being born again and of Jesus Christ as my personal Saviour grew as I grew spiritually, until one day when I was delivering a sermon from the altar of our church in Pasadena, I realized that if I had been the only sinner on earth, God would still have sent his Son into incarnation to save my soul. With the realization of so great a love that God should send his Son so that I should be restored to eternal life, I was filled with the Holy Spirit. Waves upon waves of his love filled my soul. Therefore I bear witness to a personal conversion and a personal walk with Jesus Christ.

20

Love

IN THE TENTH grade, I had a déjà vu experience. There was a boy in my school whose name was Vladimir. He had a Russian mother and a Yugoslav father, and they had emigrated from Yugoslavia. He was two years older than me.

I first saw Vladimir when he was looking through the window of a door to a classroom where I was sitting. Looking at his face, I knew him instantly, and it was love at first sight. In my soul I was passionately attached to him.

By and by I met Vladimir. He would visit me and my mother and talk about Europe, European politics and similar things. We had a record player in the living room, and I taught him ballroom dancing. He was a good dancer; he had a sense of rhythm.

When he was graduating from high school, I felt that since I had taught him to dance, he owed it to me to take me to the senior prom. But it didn't seem like that was going to happen. So I went out into my garden and I made a fiat to God for divine justice in this situation. I delivered all the power and fire of my being to God to resolve this.

Then I walked in from the garden to the house, the telephone rang, and it was Vladimir on the phone. He invited me to the senior prom and I was thrilled.

I went shopping for a dress and found a beautiful gown made of a fabric that had a design of blue flowers. It had straps, a little chiffon arrangement over the bust line and a royal blue ribbon at the center. It was in an upscale shop that sold expensive clothes and it was quite costly.

I went back and I looked at this dress every day. It cost more than I had ever paid for a dress. My mother and I had made most of my clothes up to that time, but she decided to buy it for me, and I was very happy that I had this beautiful dress to wear.

The prom was at the exclusive Berkeley Carteret Hotel in Asbury Park. It was a sit-down dinner banquet and a dance. I don't particularly remember dancing, but I know we did. Vladimir took me to the dance and took me home. It was basically uneventful. Somehow my expectations had been greater than reality.

For maybe a year I had had a crush on this boy, and it was truly a heartthrob. I still had a crush on him and it lasted for at least another year. I was definitely enamored of him but I'm sure it wasn't mutual.

The same year as the prom, Vladimir met a Cuban girl. She was one of the most beautiful girls I had ever seen. She had a perfect complexion, beautiful blonde hair and a wonderful Cuban Spanish accent. After school in the Spanish class, she would demonstrate Spanish dances. I went one time and there was Vladimir, clapping his hands and tapping his feet while she was dancing. He was totally taken with her.

So I walked home alone, with my heart just absolutely breaking in my chest. When I got home I was still crying, and my mother was upset and my father was upset. Then my mother's friends got upset. Everybody got in the act, because I'd be cleaning house on Saturdays and I'd be crying. This was the biggest pain I had ever experienced in my life. The pain could not have been greater.

By the time I was a junior in high school, Vladimir had graduated. I think he went directly into the army. I probably heard from him now and then, and he wrote to me in my senior year when I was in Switzerland. The last time I saw him was in New York when I worked at the United Nations. I looked at him and he was just one more person that blended into the crowd. He was no longer outstanding to me in any way whatsoever.

My first love wasn't my ultimate love, and when you have a first love and your heart is broken, it seems like you never quite give that much again. I think that the people who are childhood sweethearts and finally wind up marrying, if they're truly meant for each other, are the ones who don't have broken hearts, because they have always been true to each other. I have always thought that it's an ideal situation to have married your first love. But that was not my karma in this life.

Looking back on it now, I realize that this was somebody out of my past who struck a deep emotional chord within me which was totally unexplainable. I learned later that this sudden recognition and flow of energy is typical of a relationship of karma. I don't know whether he represented a conglomerate of people I knew in a past life or whether I had known this specific lifestream. In any case, it was an experience that affected me deeply.

IN THE SUMMER of 1955, the year after I had gone to Beach
Haven with Jane, I was back there again. But this year I was
alone. Beach Haven was pristine in those days, and the area at
the southern tip of the island near the Coast Guard station
was almost deserted. Often I was the only person on this
beach with glorious white sand and warm water.

At the beach I tried to get a job as a waitress, but the
woman who ran the restaurant wouldn't hire me because
according to state law I was underage. So I found a family
who hired me to take care of their children, clean their house
and help them cook when they had guests over. I worked for
them a number of times a week. Although it didn't pay very
well, I was grateful for the job because I was trying to save
money to go to college.

I noticed that when the moon was full at Beach Haven, it
was huge. It would be suspended low in the heavens, like a
harvest moon, almost reddish-orange, a sensual moon, hanging low over the Atlantic. Under that moon, the guys from the
Coast Guard station would be out necking on the beach at
night. That's the kind of life that went on there. Long Beach
Island was full of teenagers and college kids and there was
lots of partying, drinking and sexual activity.

When I saw these young people at Beach Haven, I wished
I had a boyfriend. But that summer I never did. It was lonely
for me because I didn't fit into that crowd. Though I didn't
want to be with them, I would have liked having a boyfriend.
However, God saw to it that I didn't.

It was my profound conviction that I wanted no part of
alcohol and no part of cigarettes. I had watched my parents
smoke, almost chain smoke, day in and day out. At least three
times a week, I saw my father drink and become inebriated.
And the times he wasn't inebriated, he was on the verge of it

because he was so thin that he couldn't hold his alcohol. So it was the conviction of my soul and my inner being that I would not partake of these habits. Then, too, when I was nine years old, I went to Christian Science Sunday school and found out that Christian Scientists don't smoke or drink alcohol.

So I would go to the beach alone and I would commune with God. I had my Bible and my *Science and Health,* and that summer I read *The Song of Bernadette,* by Franz Werfel. Reading the story of the life of Saint Bernadette of Lourdes was an inspiration to me. It was the spiritual path that I desired, but it was difficult to be on a spiritual path in the midst of the social life that was going on around me. And to be on that path, I had to be alone and lonely, because the two didn't mix.

So I understand all too well how teenagers who are brought up in strict religious environments find it incompatible with their social life and the trends of the times. If they are not rooted in the very core of their being to a spiritual path, they are probably going to skip it while they are teenagers. But I was one of those who had the strength and the spiritual fire to be willing to separate myself out and be who I was at the price of not having friends. And, in fact, most of those potential friends at Beach Haven were not worth having.

I was in a family that was so dysfunctional that there was only one way to go, and that was to God. I longed for God. I yearned for God. I yearned for my mission. I couldn't wait to find out what my mission was. And to a certain extent, living in Beach Haven that summer seemed like languishing.

I loved to be in the water, I loved to go swimming, I loved to lie in the sun. But on the other hand, where was my mission? Where were my people? And what was God going to call me to do?

So I would just talk to God. I would read passages from *The Song of Bernadette* and I would talk to God. I talked to God a lot.

ONE TIME WHEN I was in high school, I got a telephone call from a girlfriend stating that three or four girlfriends were all going on blind dates and I had to come too. I had no desire or intention of going, but they were determined that I would. And so the blind date that turned up for me was somebody from Wisconsin, with a Wisconsin accent.

I had never been outside of the Northeast at that time, except when I went to Switzerland as a child, so I was quite East Coast in my culture and values. And that section of the country can be somewhat narrow in its views. Everything else was considered kind of hick and beneath the high academic and cultural standards of the East. And since that was almost all I had known, I had absorbed that attitude.

So I looked at this character from Wisconsin and his accent and his whole farm-country consciousness, and I thought, "This is the worst thing that ever happened to me." I thought he was the worst bore and the worst kind of character you could ever imagine, and I was so repulsed that I couldn't wait to get away from this situation. I felt that I had really been burned. So I came home and told my mother about this terrible individual, and I told her, "I'll *never* marry a man from Wisconsin!"

It was five or six years before I ever met anybody from Wisconsin again. And the next person I met from Wisconsin was Mark Prophet.

I think Morya was testing me out in this situation in high

school to see what would happen when this girl from the East who would go to college in the East met with this folksy guy from the Midwest who was a chela of Morya. I have sometimes wondered whether my violent reaction to this individual postponed my meeting Mark for the next five years while I grew up and realized that people with Wisconsin accents really had some value to them.

I LIVED MY life freely as an inner walk with God the best I could till I was twenty-two and met Mark Prophet. Along the course of those years, I dated, I had relationships, I had friends, I did various things, and all of these things contributed to who and what I am today.

21

Switzerland

THE MORNING OF my seventeenth birthday, April 8, 1956, was a turning point in my life. Since I was a child, I had slept in the back bedroom of our house in my little, single bed, which faced the window. The morning sun came through that window, and in the spring and summer it shone through a huge silver maple that was between our house and the neighbor's property. The birds would be singing, shafts of sunlight would come twinkling through the leaves as the breezes blew, and it was as if angels would wake me up.

I remember waking up that morning and saying to myself, "Why, I have to go to Switzerland this year." I got out of bed and ran and told my mother, "I'm supposed to go to Switzerland and study French." She said, "Well, you talk to your father about it." I told my father and he said, "Talk to your mother."

Since the age of five, I had saved my money and it had been piling up—my violets money, my pot holder money, my pincushion money and money from babysitting. So now I had enough money to pay my own way to Europe. And I had many relatives who would be happy to have me stay with them when I got there. It was my college money, but I decided I could spend it on this trip because going to Switzerland would further my education since I would become fluent in French.

I had been letting God direct me and I had woken up that day with the awareness "If you don't learn French now, you'll never learn it, because you've got a mission to do and you won't have time to learn it later." In high school I had already finished three years of French, and I had a deep sense that I had to learn to speak it fluently. But I felt that soon my life would all be laid out for me and I would have other things to do. As the years would go by, I would never have this opportunity again. This turned out to be absolutely true.

We had a family meeting and my parents decided I could go. I had the money in the bank. The principal and superintendent of schools also thought I could go. I was doing well enough in my classes that they were going to let me leave early, before the end of the school year. My mother wrote to my relatives and inquired about what schools I should attend. All the relatives got involved and decided where I should go to school and where I should live.

I left on May 28, 1956, and arrived in Kloten airport in Zurich the next day. All the relatives were waiting for me. When I stepped off the plane, I was wearing a light brown and white tweed straight skirt and jacket with a blouse underneath, and this was complemented with apricot-colored suede shoes and a matching purse. To top it off, I wore gloves and a hat with a little white feather and a veil. That's how people dressed in the 1950s.

When I saw the airport, I was impressed with how beautiful and modern it was. It had polished marble floors.

But the most memorable event was walking down the stairs in those shoes. The heels weren't too high, but they were high enough to fall in. And at age seventeen, I wasn't seaworthy in high heels. As I glided off the plane, my feet shot out from under me and I tumbled down the steps. Uncle Werner never stopped kidding me about it the whole trip.

MY MOTHER COULDN'T understand why I would want to go to Europe alone and did not want a companion, but I said, "I'll be just fine." At that age I was an explorer and I didn't have any reason to have a companion. I would go anywhere, do anything—totally fearless, totally trusting in God.

In those days it was in style to hitchhike, so I hitchhiked all over Switzerland. If I was somewhere and wanted to get somewhere else and there was no other way to go, I'd just get out in the road with my little satchel on my back and stick out my thumb. Invariably, some well-dressed businessman would pick me up and drop me off where I was going. I never thought anything of it and never worried about my safety. I had complete peace with God, faith in God, absolute trust. I didn't know anything about the bad parts of the world or anything about the world that scared me. And if there was anything bad out there, it wasn't going to be where I was. That was just the way I looked at life.

At that time I was innocent, and I think there is a certain protection in innocence itself. My aura was one of innocence, and it was probably obvious to anybody who met me, and so people didn't take advantage of me.*

When I was in Switzerland, I went to a public high school in Neuchâtel. This school had a summer course and students

---

* In 1956 it was safe to hitchhike around Europe, unlike today.

came from all over the world to study there. Languages fascinated me, so I was studying German, Spanish and Italian, and I was becoming fluent in French. I wanted to stay and study until I could become fluent in all these languages.

At the headquarters of the United Nations in Geneva, I saw how they did simultaneous interpreting and this fascinated me too. While someone is speaking, the interpreter is listening and speaking simultaneously. Geneva has a school for this, and I wanted to go there until I could do it perfectly. I desperately wanted to be a simultaneous interpreter for the United Nations.

Later I realized that this experience was related to my training to be a messenger, because simultaneous translation is similar to what a messenger is doing—receiving a message from one of the ascended masters and giving it forth simultaneously, in full conscious awareness.

But even though I wanted to stay, my parents and high-school faculty demanded that I return. I had been sent out for two months and had been there for seven, so they said I had to come home to finish what was left of my senior year in high school.

In Switzerland I studied night and day, and I did become fluent in French. So I had the real excitement of hearing myself speak in another language that wasn't my own.

WHEN I WAS staying with relatives in Switzerland, I encountered vegetarianism for the second time. Elisabeth Enkerli, my cousin, was a strict vegetarian, and she and her brothers and sisters (whose parents had died when the youngest of eight children were seven and eight years old) were all vegetarians. They prepared wonderful meals that were meat-free but full of milk, cheese and yogurt.

I especially liked the Swiss muesli that was invented by Dr. Bircher. It was made of soaked oats combined with nuts and fruits of the season, to which was added pure cream and perhaps sugar. It's a one-meal dish, and now it's eaten all over the world.

I also learned about vegetarianism from Laurie Roth, a Christian Science practitioner who was a friend of my mother's from their school days. She was probably 55 or 60 when we met and I enjoyed spending time with her. She was a great comfort while I was a boarder in the house of a strict Calvinist Protestant pastor, Monsieur Lachat, who did not approve of Christian Science.

Laurie Roth would always prepare vegetarian meals when I visited her, most of the time delicious omelets. We would feast on the omelets and feast on our meditation on the holy scriptures and the writings of Mary Baker Eddy.

WHEN I COMPLETED my studies in Switzerland, I arranged to go to Paris for two weeks on the way home. I was going to fly there, check into a hotel and just see Paris on my own. But since I was only seventeen, my Swiss relatives wouldn't hear of this. So when I got on the plane, there was my wonderful Uncle Werner. He was one of the five men who were generals in the Swiss army during the Second World War. Uncle Werner showed me Paris, and when he left, he let his business colleagues take me around. But usually I was free in the daytime.

Wearing my camel hair coat and saddle shoes, I walked around Paris, making a pilgrimage to every church I could get to in the course of ten days. I must have gone into twenty-five or thirty churches, and I went to every altar of each one. I knelt, I prayed, and I called to God for the people of the city, for peace, as well as for him to use me as his servant. I loved every church in that city.

It was the Christmas season in Paris and it was foggy and misty. Sometimes it rained. It was as if Paris was *my* city for two weeks. I went to the Île de la Cité to see the halls of justice and the courts. A nice judge befriended me, took me into the courtrooms and explained the cases and everything that was going on. I spent a lot of time right around Sainte-Chapelle and the surrounding area, and I felt that I had been there before. It felt like home turf to me.

After this judge had finished showing me around, he asked to meet me after work and take me to dinner. So I was there at five o'clock, but I started getting very scared and a great fear of this man came upon me. Looking around, I grabbed the back of a streetcar and left as fast as I could. I knew that I shouldn't be around this man anymore. As I looked back on it later, it seemed to me that this person must have been somebody I bumped into from a past life who had brought some kind of harm to me.

One of the places I went to was a huge wholesale market which occupies many blocks in a certain district of Paris. I was told that it was a sight to see in Paris, and if I wanted to see the real activity in this market, I should be there at dawn. When I got there, I walked about the market—as usual, in my camel hair coat and saddle shoes—wondering, as always, why everybody thought I was an American, not realizing that my coat and shoes were totally giving it away.

As I walked through the place, I saw vast quantities of vegetables, fruits and flowers. The flower part of the market was tremendous, an abundance of magnificent cut flowers.

Then all of a sudden I came upon a huge section that sold meat. Whole carcasses of cows, pigs, lambs, chickens and every other kind of meat were hanging from racks—a solid wall of meat. It was the first time in my life I had ever seen a wholesale meat market or any kind of market where there was anything but precut meat prepared and packaged for household consumption. And then and there I said to myself, "I cannot eat meat anymore."

From that day forward I did not eat meat for a number of years. But without any understanding of the science of a vegetarian diet and simply eating everything on the table except the meat, I discovered that I was not feeling well and I was gaining weight. Finally I came to the conclusion that I was not suited to being a vegetarian and I was not healthy on this diet. So little by little I began eating fish and then meat again.

MY TIME IN Europe contributed a great deal to my growing up and my maturity. For at seventeen, I went there alone. I got on a plane, flew alone and traveled all over Switzerland alone. With train passes I rode all over the place and did a lot of hitchhiking around the country. I was on my own and had to completely manage my own life. If I didn't get up in the morning, nobody got me up. If I didn't study, nobody was there to tell me to study. Nobody was there to tell me what to eat, how to live, who to hang around with or what to do. The journey was an expression of independence.

But even more than this, when I flew home from Paris on a rainy December day in 1956, I brought back a message that has stayed in my heart ever since. It was the year of the Hungarian uprising, when Hungarians were fighting against Soviet tanks with their bare hands and their bodies, and more than two thousand were killed. The nations were outraged, yet the United States, the great defender of freedom, did not come to the Hungarians' aid, because to do so would have meant a direct confrontation with the Soviet Union. So instead of coming to the aid of people fighting for freedom, we stood by and let not only Hungary but later Czechoslovakia be dealt with in this manner.

I remember going to the demonstrations that were taking place in the streets of Neuchâtel. I remember the candlelight vigils for the Hungarian refugees, whom Switzerland, as a neutral nation, was receiving. I remember the support and welcome Switzerland gave to the Hungarian freedom fighters and the demonstrations that occurred simultaneously around the world.

The brutal destruction of the spirit of a people by the Soviets was burned in my soul. It was an unforgettable moment in my life, one that I believe shaped, in part, my future and my mission.

22

Other Realms

ONE DAY MY Sunday school teacher asked the class, "Who wants to be a Christian Science practitioner when you grow up?" Immediately I raised my hand. It was not a decision of the moment. I had thought about it a long time. I thought the most glorious thing in the whole wide world that anybody could do was to heal people, and I wanted to follow in the footsteps of Mary Baker Eddy.

I was already praying for the sick in the way that I was taught to do in Christian Science—by affirming the absolute God-good where the appearance of sin, disease or death was present and by denying the power of error, or evil, to create that appearance or any manifestation that was not God-good. Of all the people I knew then, those whom I respected most and saw as role models were the Christian Science practitioners, especially Mrs. Schofield. Their love and their devotion to God and to their calling impressed me. I wanted to help people less fortunate than I, and I saw scientific prayer as the greatest power available to me at that stage of my spiritual development.

As the years passed, my prayers became more effective and more powerful. I began praying for the healing of souls. I asked my Sunday school teacher if I could visit Christian Scientists who were bedridden to read to them from the Bible and *Science and Health,* to comfort them and to affirm the truth concerning their condition. One of the church members drove me to the homes of the elderly who were bedridden. My visits made them happy and made me happy too.

I partook of the Word of God by reading Christian Science texts and the scriptures and by meditating on the law that God had written in my inward parts.[28] And I listened to the voice of God that spoke with a quality of unspeakable love, of wisdom I had never heard with the outer ear but only with the inner ear. It was a presence so powerful as to render impotent the lesser voices of the night.

The Word, the love and the law of God were my Holy Communion, and I celebrated this Communion daily. I read in the Book of John, "Except ye eat the flesh of the Son of man, and drink his blood, ye have no life in you."[29] Even then I knew that the flesh and blood of Jesus Christ were the light-essence of the Father-Mother God and that I must assimilate the spiritual sustenance of the Body and Blood of my Lord.

I knew from the Old Testament that the name of God was I AM THAT I AM,[30] so I took note of the statements of Jesus that began with the name of God—I AM the bread of life; I AM the light of the world; I AM the door of the sheep; I AM the good shepherd; I AM the resurrection and the life; I AM the way, the truth and the life; I AM the vine, ye are the branches.[31]

About this time I read another book that inspired my faith. It was Norman Vincent Peale's *The Power of Positive Thinking for Young People.* He also used the name I AM and included I AM affirmations in his book.

Wherever I discovered a principle or a law in the words and works of Jesus, I affirmed by the name of God I AM that that principle or that law was active in me. Then I looked for Jesus' "I" statements—such as: I and my Father are one; I can of mine own self do nothing ... but the Father that dwelleth in me, he doeth the works; my Father worketh hitherto, and I work; I must work the works of him that sent me, while it is day: the night cometh, when no man can work.[32] In all humility I affirmed the applicability of these statements in my life, for I believed with all my heart that Jesus intended me and every Christian to follow in his footsteps. For had he not said: "He that believeth on me, the works that I do shall he do also; and greater works than these shall he do; because I go unto my Father"?[33]

I also took Mary Baker Eddy's statements of the scientific affirmation of Christ-truth and affirmed these as active within me, as a leaven of light in my consciousness. By this means I sought to bring myself closer and closer in attunement with the mind of God.

The command of the apostle "Let this mind be in you, which was also in Christ Jesus"[34] rang in my heart like cathedral bells chiming the cadences of the mind of God. If God wants me to let the mind of Christ be in me, and if I accept it and allow it and acclaim it, then that mind must become my mind, and my mind must become the agency of the mind of God. Then, at the point of the merging of the two minds, there can be no duality but only one mind.

I saw everyone as a potential extension of the mind of God. I saw that we all could dip into that universal intelligence. And as we did so, we would be extensions of that intelligence, even as sunbeams are extensions of the Great Sun Source.

I DIDN'T MAKE a fetish of Christian Science, but I pursued the practice of it with all my heart. It was my rock of Truth. But I had also come to Christian Science having already acquired my own worldview, which included the doctrines of karma and reincarnation, the continuity of the soul, and the sense that I had lived before and would continue to coexist with God in this life and beyond.

Christian Scientists deny karma and reincarnation, but I solidly, firmly, profoundly believed in karma and reincarnation from the time I began to think. From the time I began to have cognition, I knew that I antedated the body I was in. Those were givens. Those were a priori awarenesses that I had without ever having to be taught. And when my mother told me that I had remembered a past life, I agreed with her because some part of me already knew that. She was simply articulating it and conceptualizing it for me and giving me a rationale regarding the justice of God.

I also believed that there were angels who taught and comforted God's children and nature spirits who tended the earth and the seasons as God's gardeners and our helpers. I sensed beings of light, masterful presences and saints just beyond the veil that limited my vision into the unseen world. Yet Christian Scientists denied their existence.

I did not see the Spirit cosmos and the Matter cosmos as separate, but matter as a step down, and many steps down in vibration, from the highest frequencies of God's light beyond physical measuring. I saw that when the spin of matter decelerated to a certain level, it was subject to cycles of disintegration, dissolution and—in the case of human, animal and plant life—death. Therefore, when I affirmed the unreality of matter, I was affirming the nonpermanence of all that could not sustain itself independently of God or Spirit. And that which could not hold permanency could not hold reality; hence it was unreal.

Whenever I was called upon to read the scriptures or lead the Lord's Prayer, I felt the immediate tie to God's Presence and to our Lord. It was my highest calling and my most meaningful experience in both public school and Sunday school. And when I was alone in my bedroom, apart from household chores and homework, I was in another dimension as I read the Bible and the writings of Mary Baker Eddy and, as a senior in high school, the sayings of the Buddha. In that contemplation of the Word of God and the truth which Christ brought to free us from our mortality, I knew the universality of all true religion.

I found in Mary Baker Eddy the free spirit that I also was, unconfined in her understanding of the eternal truth that she discovered. But I found that some Christian Scientists have a narrow, mentalistic approach to practicing Christian Science healing and to understanding the doctrine of Jesus Christ, which Mary Baker Eddy demonstrated best by her example.

Jesus had spoken the words to my heart, "I am the open door which no man can shut," and I knew that no one could shut the door to Jesus' heart that my Lord had opened to me unless I allowed them to. Yet when I took up the study of Eastern religions—including Buddhism, Hinduism, the sayings of Confucius and the way of Lao Tzu—I was told in no uncertain terms that I should not read these books. For according to the Christian Science *Manual of the Mother Church,* "As adherents of Truth, we take the inspired Word of the Bible as our sufficient guide to eternal Life."[35]

Since I understood many things concerning God's law and his love and his presence with me, I decided to follow the Mother of Jesus, who "kept all these things and pondered them in her heart."[36] For I loved Christian Science, I loved the church, I loved my Sunday school teachers, the practitioners and the members. And I knew I had much to learn from them, for I was but a child.

ONE DAY I opened *Science and Health,* and my eyes fell upon these words from the heart of my beloved leader: "The Soul-inspired patriarchs heard the voice of Truth, and talked with God as consciously as man talks with man."[37] Then and there I knew that Mary Baker Eddy had talked with God and that my own walking and talking with God was justified by her experience today as well as that of the patriarchs and prophets of yesterday. And others, even in this day and age, are also having this experience.

One day I prayed to Jesus to know what mystery he would reveal to me. I asked him to direct me to the text in Mrs. Eddy's writings that would open a door. It was as though the Master had his hand on the doorknob ready to open the door and I had but to ask. With a sense of anticipation, I picked up *Science and Health* and let it fall open where it would. It was the conclusion of Mrs. Eddy's "Key to the Scriptures." Her statement was that Saint John's vision in Revelation "is the acme of this Science [Christian Science] as the Bible reveals it."[38]

Eagerly I opened the Book of Revelation at random, aware of the Master's closeness. I read chapter 7:

> After this I beheld, and, lo, a great multitude, which
> no man could number, of all nations, and kindreds,
> and people, and tongues, stood before the throne, and
> before the Lamb, clothed with white robes, and palms

in their hands;

And cried with a loud voice, saying, Salvation to our God which sitteth upon the throne, and unto the Lamb.

And all the angels stood round about the throne, and about the elders and the four beasts, and fell before the throne on their faces, and worshipped God.

Saying, Amen: Blessing, and glory, and wisdom, and thanksgiving, and honour, and power, and might, be unto our God for ever and ever. Amen.

And one of the elders answered, saying unto me, What are these which arc arrayed in white robes? and whence came they?

And I said unto him, Sir, thou knowest. And he said to me, These are they which came out of great tribulation, and have washed their robes, and made them white in the blood of the Lamb.

Therefore are they before the throne of God, and serve him day and night in his temple: and he that sitteth on the throne shall dwell among them.

They shall hunger no more, neither thirst any more; neither shall the sun light on them, nor any heat.

For the Lamb which is in the midst of the throne shall feed them, and shall lead them unto living fountains of waters: and God shall wipe away all tears from their eyes.[39]

I was ready to know the mystery of the saints robed in white. I read these verses three times and smiled the smile of spiritual gladness. For I had been feeling the presence of beings of "whiteness" whom I had only glimpsed in shafts of light like sunbeams. I felt their love and companionship.

These friends of the Spirit were not astral, shadowed forms of lower worlds. They were in the glory of the Lord. They were friends I had known before and would know again. The concrete barriers of time and space could not keep them from me.

The veil was thinning. The time-space reference of my life was but a band of consciousness that marched through timeless, spaceless realms of heaven in 4/4 time. And heaven was all around me, up and down and sideways. These souls, the "saints robed in white," were free in the light of Christ. Some of them would go out no more, would never again descend through the tunnel of incarnation. For they had washed their robes and made them white in the blood of the Lamb. Others were scheduled to return once more to finish the unfinished work of the Lord on earth.

I was happy in a universe teeming with life, for I was a part of that life. I leaned back from my desk to ponder what I had read and what I had seen. For as John had written it, in that moment as I read it, I was seeing it. And as I leaned back, my eyes passed through and beyond the floral pattern on my yellow wallpaper. I was in another dimension.

I thought about a recent experience when I was waterskiing down the Navesink River. Hugh, a Christian Scientist I had met at church, had taken me out in his boat and I had skied all afternoon. How I had enjoyed that freedom of movement, gliding over the water, that salt air and sunshine and, for a few hours, that sense of not having a care in the cosmos. As we approached a bridge, the water got choppy. I made up my mind to stay on those skis, so I focused on the water with a determined eye, locked in and did it.

As we passed under the bridge, I passed into another plane. I was aware that my focus in the next plane was just as sharp as it had been in this plane when I had been measuring those waves and my response to them a moment before. I was not daydreaming. I was alert and in full possession of my faculties, even of those soul faculties that now and again had taken me outside the boundaries of my day-to-day world.

Still on my skis, I was suspended in a place where spiritual beings dwelt. They were aware of me as I was aware of them. They were joyous in the light. They radiated love. Though they seemed to be above me at a distance, yet there was no distance. Our auras touched. Their joy and light passed into me, and I remember saying, "Why are you there and why am I here? What is the mission?"

There was no other communication. The parting of the veil, the opening of a door and the contact was all there was. But that "all" was a slice of eternity that would last me a lifetime. My horizons were no longer limited by the rising and the setting sun, but only by the cycles of heaven's appearing.

RETURNING TO THE revelation at hand and comparing it to my encounter on the river, I took up my concordance to *Science and Health* and the works of Mary Baker Eddy. I looked up all of her references to "beings" and "immortals"; I wanted to know everything my teacher had to say on the subject. Perhaps I could find in her writings some point of comparison between her experience and mine.

I found more than I had expected, and I gained insight into the spiritual reality that was a part of her world. In *Science and Health* she wrote: "Advancing spiritual steps in the teeming universe of Mind lead on to spiritual spheres and *exalted beings.*"[40] "Mortals will disappear, and *immortals, or the children of God,* will appear as the only and eternal verities of man."[41] "The universe of Spirit is peopled with

139

spiritual beings, and its government is divine Science."[42]

In these statements I had the confirmation that I was on firm ground. Mrs. Eddy did not write an intellectual treatise; of that I was certain. She wrote the statement of her direct experience with God and his divine science. The application of that divine science to the world in which we live she named Christian Science. But she did not commit to writing all of the mysteries that God and Jesus Christ had revealed to her. Some of the truths were given only to advanced students or her household staff.[43] Others she communicated to no one.

Mrs. Eddy's testimony of the Science of Mind was her direct experience with that science. When she spoke of "the teeming universe of Mind," she was not offering a mere hypothesis. She was attesting to her direct awareness of spiritual spheres and exalted beings. When she spoke of "immortals, or the children of God," she was making a statement of her own experience. When she said, "The universe of Spirit is peopled with spiritual beings," she placed before her students the glorious panorama of the planes of heaven to which souls advance as they graduate from earth's schoolroom.

The spiritual beings and the government of divine science were known to Mary Baker Eddy. I believe that before she passed on, she had already entered that world, and ultimately she did join the ranks of the immortals who had visited her during her earthly mission. They comforted her through her trials and tribulations as they have comforted the saints throughout the ages.

Today I know that these saints robed in white, whom John the Revelator revealed, are the ascended masters. They are the sons and daughters of God who make up the company of saints robed in white, whom Jesus revealed to Mrs. Eddy just as he had revealed them to John.

I also bear witness to this mystery of the kingdom. For on that day, in the golden glow of my room, Jesus opened the door and revealed to me the actuality of Revelation—and the actuality of Mrs. Eddy's confirmation of this scripture. And I am convinced that this vision can and will come to any disciple of Christ-truth who will incline his inner ear and his heart, his spiritual vision and his soul faculties to the realities of God that are all around us, even pressing in upon us.

Mrs. Eddy's own advancing spiritual steps in the teeming universe of mind led her to the feet of her I AM Presence, as she revealed in her poem "Christ and Christmas":

> For Christian Science brings to view
> The great I Am,—
> Omniscient power,—gleaming through
> Mind, mother, man.[44]

Thus she saw that God is no respecter of persons, that the great I AM as the omniscient power of the Almighty manifests through male and female. The I AM Presence is personified for each one, providing intimate and unceasing communion with God.

BEFORE I FINISHED high school, I had another experience in which my spiritual senses were heightened. It was a beautiful sunny day and I was on my weekly walk to Sunday school. I was praising God in the words of the Psalmist:

> Praise ye the LORD. Praise ye the LORD from the heavens: praise him in the heights.
> Praise ye him, all his angels: praise ye him, all his

hosts.

Praise ye him, sun and moon: praise him, all ye stars of light.

Praise him, ye heavens of heavens, and ye waters that be above the heavens.

Let them praise the name of the LORD: for he commanded, and they were created.[45]

As I said these words, gently I was being lifted, perhaps on the wings of my song of praise, to the realm of light whose door had been opened to me by Jesus. Beyond the sky and clouds, I saw, in my soul—I don't know what other phrase to use—"a multitude of the heavenly host."[46]

By the time I arrived at the church parking lot, I was inundated with an overwhelming joy. My friend Dick Fontaine was just getting out of his station wagon. I remember exclaiming to him, "Dick, something wonderful is going to happen in my life!"

I thought to myself that this must be a special day. It was as though all of the visible sky was filled with numberless numbers of angels and bright spirits who were praising God, and I had been allowed to witness the glory of God that was upon them.

Yet it was so personal. Again, they all knew me and I knew them. Again, it was the parting of the veil and the contact with other realms. The joy and the glory of the Lord was with me for days. As I write, I am thrilled anew by the mere touching of the record of this momentous occasion in my life. That day in Sunday school I was distracted from the lesson as I pondered the why and the wherefore. I came to the conclusion that the gift of God to me that Sunday was the promise of the mission. The words of the hymn were in my heart: "The earth shall be filled with the glory of God / As the waters cover the sea."[47]

I had never doubted, from the time I was conscious of having a thought process, that God had called me to a mission and that he who had called me would fulfill what he had purposed to do through me. I believed that God's teaching would go forth and that God's own would have a mighty victory. I had the sense of an about-to-happen great glory.

On that day I was strengthened in my one-pointedness in preparing for the goal. I didn't have to know exactly what the mission would be, but I knew that I had to prepare for it. For when it was ready for me, I had to be ready for it.

AROUND GRADUATION TIME, when my life in Red Bank was drawing to a close, I had one final experience of other realms. One Sunday morning I was standing on the church steps after the service as the congregation and children were milling about. I was filled with the light that I had become accustomed to receiving Sunday after Sunday. Suddenly, I found myself turning around abruptly toward one of the pillars, even as I said aloud to myself, "Why, I have to make my ascension in this life!"

The power of those words came upon me as a fiat of the Lord. I couldn't believe what I had said. Christian Science had never taught me that I or anyone else was to "ascend," in that specific terminology. When I spoke the words, simultaneously I knew what they meant, though I had not been taught their meaning—not on my mother's knee, not by Mrs. Schofield and not at Sunday school.

For uncounted moments I was riveted to the spot. I felt the presence of an emissary of God and a power that was awesome.[48] I accepted the decree of the Lord for my life. It was as though I had been repolarized to the Polestar of my Being, the Great I AM. Now I knew the end of the mission. To arrive at that destination, I would have to find out how to go about making my ascension in this life.

MY LIFE IN Red Bank would soon be ending. I saw it as a prologue that would soon be the past. Imminently, I thought, chapter one must begin.

But just how imminent was to be the encounter that would send me on my search I did not know.

23

Saint Germain

AFTER GRADUATING FROM high school, the world was at my doorstep, and I was about to step off into a life of new opportunities and exciting people. It was September 1957, and I was ready to go to New York City to catch the train to college. But I wondered, "Before I leave, is there anything in this house in Red Bank that would help me on my way?" I was sure I wouldn't be coming back.

As I stood in the library, I prayed to God and said, "Dear God, thank you for my parents, my home, my schooling and all that you have given me. If there is anything that you have placed here for me, for my benefit, which I have not availed myself of, please tell me, because I'm leaving and I'm not coming back."

I didn't expect the thunderous reply that I received. As soon as I offered that prayer, the voice of God was in my temple, in my very bosom, and it was speaking to me and giving me a direct order: "Go to that bookcase, pick up that book and read it." I knew very well what "that book" was. It was a book I had seen on the shelf since childhood, and I was afraid of that book. It was like a book of energy sitting there, and I felt that if I happened to pick it up, it would change my life. Throughout my childhood I would walk around it and look at it and then tiptoe away. And yet I would always be drawn back to it. It was a magnet.

I said to myself, "Now you're in for it! You've asked, you've been told, you can't disobey. So go and get that book." So I went and got the book, *The "I AM" Discourses,* by Godfré Ray King. I thought it would probably take me all day to understand what was in it, so I sank down into an old leather chair with my legs over the arm and opened the book.

Before I even came to the text, I saw a portrait of a master, whom I recognized instantly. I looked into that face and it was as though the eyes were talking to me. I recognized him, though I had never seen anything like it before. I read the name underneath, Saint Germain.

As I looked into his eyes, that face became alive and quickened. I was meeting one I had always known. I had tapped into a soul memory, recognizing him as probably the oldest friend I had ever known.

I leaped out of that chair about two feet and ran to my mother in the kitchen. I said, "Mother, Saint Germain! I know him. I've got to find him. I've got a work to do for him. Do you know him?"

She said, "Yes, I know him."

I said, "Mother, why didn't you ever tell me about him?"

She said, "I wanted you to discover him for yourself."

"Well," I thought to myself, "eighteen years of wasted life. Here it is, I finally found him. I wonder if she was going to wait till I was eighty-five to tell me about Saint Germain." And so I said, "Well, I've got to go out and find him."

IN THE MOMENT that my soul memory had been quickened, as I looked into Saint Germain's eyes, I recalled an experience that I had before entering this life.

I was standing in a great judgment hall before a bar of seven beings of light of beautiful stature. They were robed in white. Their eyes were profound, and their expressions contained the depths of ancient wisdom, of immense compassion. They seemed to span the centuries as emissaries of God to his children on earth.

I was standing before the bar and they were in a semicircle before me. Saint Germain was standing to my right, exactly as he was in the painting in the book. Behind me were others of the ascended masters. It was an important ceremony.

I was standing in my full consciousness and I understood that these were emissaries of God. I had come before them to review what would happen in this lifetime—the family I would be born into, the religion, place and country, the karma I was bringing with me and the karma I would be required to balance, what the mission would be, what the offering of my life in the community would be.

I heard myself saying, "Saint Germain, I vow to go to earth and bring your teaching to God's people." After I made that solemn promise, Saint Germain placed his hand upon my head and blessed me. Then I remember entering a fiery vortex of light, like a tornado, and the veil of forgetfulness descended over me, making me forget who I was before, making me forget the solemn ceremony I had just witnessed, until I recalled it eighteen years later in the library of my parents' home.

The event I recalled is something every person must go through before embodying again on earth. When the veil of forgetfulness descends over us at birth, we no longer have the

147

recall of our past lives or the purpose of our new embodiment. Most of us do not remember. I did not remember except for the master Saint Germain showing me.

For the next five years after I saw his picture in the book, I searched for Saint Germain on the outer. Inwardly, I walked and talked with him, as I was wont to do with Jesus Christ— one at the right hand, one at the other.

I had a real living relationship with these masters, and I found that all hell would break loose to oppose this relationship and to intrude other relationships and individuals upon me. I found that with the presence of other people around me, in a second I could forget my relationship with the ascended masters. All of a sudden I would realize that for fifteen minutes or a half an hour I hadn't thought of Saint Germain or Jesus, and I was more conscious of physical beings than I was of spiritual beings.

I remember walking around New York City visualizing Saint Germain on one hand and Jesus on the other. I was definitely communicating to them, and one fine day they answered back.

24

Antioch College

IN THE SPRING of 1957 I was accepted to Pembroke College at Brown University, Douglass College at Rutgers, and Antioch College. I should have made it my business to get to Brown, but I didn't think my parents would be able to swing it financially. It was too expensive. One of the terrible memories of my youth is when I was sitting in class one day and the school secretary came to the door and said, "Brown University is on the phone for you. Will you come and take the call?" And I said no.

I had so little hope. I thought there was no way I was going to be able to attend Brown University. My parents weren't going to pay for it. So I didn't even try; I didn't even apply for a scholarship. This is the burden I was under, and I think that the angels must have wept and the masters must not have known what to do because of my state of consciousness. I felt so beaten down by the circumstances of my life.

The best scholarship offer I got was from Antioch College in Yellow Springs, Ohio. All that I had ever heard about Antioch College was that it was founded by Horace Mann and that it had a co-op system.

They believed in working off campus as part of your education to find out what you wanted to be, to mature, to be responsible and to take part in community life. You would get a co-op job in whatever you wanted to major in. For example, if you wanted to be a doctor, in your freshman year you could be an orderly in a hospital. Businesses all over the country participated in the program, and Antioch sent them people to fill their positions twelve months out of the year. So I thought, "This is great. I'm going to Antioch."

When I got to Antioch, I realized that these people were not my people. I felt I had made a mistake in going there the minute I arrived, because it was a beatnik crowd, liberal to the extreme, falling-off-the-table left wing. I could have called up Brown University and said, "I made a mistake. Can I transfer for my second semester?" But I was so conditioned to feel bad about myself, I didn't do it.

I felt like I was almost the only girl on campus who had any religion and who would not participate in the immorality of campus life that was so rampant there. I felt that that life was fine for them if they wanted it, but it wasn't for me. And even though I had little self-esteem, I think I knew who I was and where I was going, and I was able to stand up against the crowd.

So I became a recluse. I lived a monastic life in the midst of an extremely liberal campus, and I made up my mind what I was there for. I worked in the basement of the library in the stacks, I studied night and day, I took an extra load of courses and did about three years work in two. For there was no point in entering into the type of social life that was going on there.

Most people I met at Antioch did not believe in God, and quite a few upperclassmen attempted to convince me that there was no God. Of course I had a profound belief in God. I remember walking out into the snow alone one night, looking up into the stars and attempting to conceive of a cosmos without God. I put my feet in the footprints of those who could experience a universe without God.

This was the first time in my life that I had done this, because for as long as I had ever been, I had known of the presence of God. But I changed the dial of my consciousness and imagined this. There I was, suspended alone in an infinite cosmos as far as the stars could be seen and beyond, and there was no God.

I walked about in that mind-set for a while and I saw the absurdity of it. And the sense of the void and the nothingness without God's presence was truly, to me, proof in itself that there was a God. This experience was profound. It was as though God was allowing me to experience all that exists without him and to see what it would be like. So I turned off that dial and was back where I always had been, in the infinite past and the infinite future, centered in the omnipresence of God.

I had my trial by fire and all of my tests at Antioch College. And I passed them without knowing I was passing them.

ACADEMICALLY, ANTIOCH COLLEGE is well known for its innovation in higher education. I remember an experimental course in geology in which I was with the group that had to learn the course on its own, without a professor. I had come from a traditional type of school, being presented information and giving it back on tests. At Antioch I learned the great joy of discovering all kinds of information in the various fields of history, literature, science, physics, and so forth, in a method of education where it was up to the individual to determine his own pursuit of knowledge and his own development of the course. On my own, without an instructor, I had the joy of learning from the book and the laboratory experiments and therefore contacting the inner teacher.

Sometimes I was impatient that I had to be self-taught and that the burden of learning was being put back on me when I was paying for an education. But I realize now that my freshman year in that school was one of the greatest liberations I had ever known thus far in life. The independence and the individuality of the student were recognized, and I was able to regain what perhaps I had not fully had as a child between the ages of two and seven.

AT ANTIOCH I had a good friend who was my German professor. His home was a place where students would go to talk and for social gatherings. I remember speaking with him one day in his office at a time when I was putting a lot of effort into German and telling him that I was studying and yet feeling that I was not excelling as much as I ought to be. He told me about a student he had who would come to his office and had read every German book on the shelf. I thought to myself, "Well, I certainly don't study German that hard." And he said to me, "You know this is not your major. This is not the thing to which you are ready to give your life."

As he said this to me, I looked at his shelves and realized in my heart, "He's right. I can't give my life to being an expert in German. It's just not me." That made me start thinking. Well, what is it that I can pour my life into? What is it that means more to me than anything else in the world?

My conclusion was that it was God. Some way or another, I had to serve God.

When I was preparing to go to college and trying to determine my major, I was considering majoring in music, art or languages. However, I realized, "Here are these things that I can do. But what difference does it make if I can do them? I can see the end from the beginning. If I go through these courses, I'll get my degree and have a career. But so what? I might be famous or I might not, but I won't be fulfilled."

At that time I would talk to God a great deal about everything—what I was doing, how I could serve him and how I could find out more of the plan and the teaching. So one day I was talking with God about what my major in college should be, and he said, "I want you to major in political science and economics."

I said, "Political science? What am I going to do with a major in political science?"

And he said, "You have to understand the governments and the economies of the nations. You have to understand what's going on in the world, because the world is heading for a very severe crisis. And until the problems of the governments and the economies are resolved, there is no point in you becoming a musician or an artist or a linguist, because we need action in the battle and on the front line."

So I thought, "Well, if that is what God needs, that's what I'll do." So I majored in political science and economics. These subjects were certainly not easy for me. They were difficult courses, but I realized that this was something that was needed. I had to have the understanding of what was happening in the world in order to fulfill my mission.

I took the courses I was told to take by the inner voice of God. I studied hard. But I also had my moments of great discouragement and of wondering, "What is all this for? It's so much useless learning." So in order to survive, I had to approach the subject matter through the mind of God. I had to keep one side of my notebook for what the professor was saying and the other side for what the voice of God was saying. I would allow God to be my teacher and tutor me. And the wondrous revelations that God would give to me on any subject I was taking, whether it was mathematics or social sciences or economics, kept me afloat. It was not only inspiring, but I was being fed manna from the mind of God while my soul was starving in the lowlands of the mental plane on which people were trying to keep me.

DURING THE TIME I was at Antioch College, I found out that I had led a sheltered life in Red Bank, New Jersey. It's a small town, and I hardly left it at all except when I went to Beach Haven and to Switzerland and spent two summers in Maine. I had never even seen Philadelphia or all the landmarks of American history that were only sixty miles from my house. My parents never even drove me there for the weekend to see Independence Hall.

Even though I might regret that I didn't go to Brown University and have the typical Ivy League experience, I would have been sheltered at Brown also. And if I had been sitting in Providence, Rhode Island, I wouldn't have gone to Boston, I wouldn't have met Mark Prophet. I wouldn't have had the accumulation of experiences that matured me a great deal in my college years.

Even though these things led to me becoming disillusioned with the world, during those years I was fast and furiously having experiences with all kinds of people I met at the U.N.

and in my other co-op jobs. Now I can see that I was being exposed to everything under the sun in this period so that I would get a clear picture of what that world was, what I would be leaving, the challenges that were in that world, and what I had to work toward. And it turned out that there was only a short time for me to be in the world before I began my training as a messenger.

When I was in high school, I would look at the homes in Rumson, New Jersey, and think, "Wouldn't it be wonderful to marry an attorney, live in Rumson and be near the beach and have a boat and bring up my kids." It was the only life I knew at that time.

But that is not the way my life turned out. And I wouldn't have been very happy if I had done that. I probably would have ended up divorcing whomever I married in that social scene. So I am happy with the life I lived and the experiences I had. For I believe that all my experiences contributed something to my becoming an adult and being able to be content with my life of service.

IN MY FIRST year of college, I read Mohandas Gandhi's book *The Story of My Experiments with Truth*. When I first read this book, I was so impressed by how candid this man was. He recorded everything he could remember about himself.

This is why Gandhi is so loved, because he paints the portrait of a human being. He paints the portrait of someone who is passing through the experiences that we all have, and he becomes real. He's not a god; he's a human being, like all of us. And because he overcame and he led an entire nation by his fastidious dedication to truth, we have some hope in our own lives, even though we may have had these problems.

You also see in this book a life that he lives because he discovers truth and he acts on it. He does not just sit there philosophizing about the truth or reading books about it. He doesn't say, "I'm going to live my private life. I'm going to do my thing. I'm not going to take any responsibility for any organization or any movement." Whatever comes into his awareness that he believes in, he must take action for millions of people.

In later years I learned from the masters that Gandhi's karma had been set aside in that life for an incarnation of world service. This is why Gandhi does not emerge as a saint in the most hallowed sense of the word, like Ramakrishna, for example. His was a path of karma yoga, and his karma wasn't balanced enough to propel him to those spiritual heights the Hindus recognize in an avatar, an incarnation of God.

Gandhi had a heavy karma. It got set aside, and he came into that life and performed his mission to perfection. By that mission, he balanced a great deal of karma, but not all, and therefore he did not make his ascension but returned into embodiment to balance the karma that had been set aside.

WHILE I WAS at Antioch, I outlined the affirmations in *The "I AM" Discourses*. I would say the words as an affirmation and repeat it with great intensity in my feeling world. That's all I knew to do. I had no knowledge of the step-up of the decree or its acceleration in what I know today as the Science of the Spoken Word. But I put myself on a course of daily doing certain exercises from this book, and I noticed a stupendous change in my life when I would do it.

This was difficult to do in a dorm with other students, with the burden of classes and other activities, and no one else around me who understood this path. I did it for a while, didn't do it for a while, picked it up again, and so forth. But this was the beginning of my application of the law of the spoken Word, and I noticed its powerful effects. It was an amazing experience.

In my freshman year at Antioch, I had an experience with the Word which was so powerful that it was almost frightening. I needed to get home for Christmas, but I didn't have a ride and I hadn't made any plans for how I was going to get home. I had thought I was going to stay at Antioch through the Christmas vacation, but I decided, no, I had to go home to New Jersey as quickly as I could get there.

I was standing in the street somewhere in Yellow Springs and I burst into a prayer: "O God, get me out of this place, and get me out of here today. I have to get home!" There was a fire in my heart that simply leaped in those words.

Then I returned to the dormitory to pack my things. No sooner had an hour passed when I walked out of my room into the hall. Someone yelled up the stairwell, "Anybody going to New Jersey? Anybody need a ride?" I said to myself, "That's it. He's here to take me home." And so I said, "I'm going to New Jersey. You can take me."

The girls in my dorm were horrified. They said, "What? Are you crazy? You're going to travel from here to New Jersey with a total stranger? You don't know this person!"

He was in the air force and he had driven up from Wright-Patterson Air Force Base. I had hardly slept for three or four days since I was taking finals, and I hadn't had a shower either. I climbed into the back seat, lay down and slept. He stopped at various Howard Johnsons on the way and brought me orange juice. I'd wake up, drink the juice and go back to sleep. I slept all the way from Antioch to the door of my house in Red Bank. Somewhere along the way he asked me to go to bed with him, and I told him I didn't do that. So he respected that and just drove me home.

God had sent him to take me home and I was there in twenty-two hours. He drove nonstop. My father looked at me when I arrived home with this soldier. He didn't like that too much. I was only eighteen at the time.

When I thought about this experience, I was frightened, because I had called to God and the manifestation of the answer was so clear. There was a power in the universe and that power responded.

It wasn't that I didn't know that God was an ever-present, loving being in my life. But I was beginning to see that there was a force, a power, an energy and a science involved. Somehow, when the fire welled up within me with such intensity, it seemed to create a fountain that would reach God, God would arc his energy back, and the matrix I had sent forth would instantly be fulfilled.

I knew that I was standing in the presence of a tremendous power, and I began to think how very near that power is and what that power could do when mankind discovered it. This was the beginning of the formulation in my heart of the Science of the Spoken Word.

25

Summer Camp

AFTER MY FIRST year at Antioch College, I took a co-op job in the summer of 1958 as a camp counselor in Vermont. École Champlain was a summer camp for girls whose parents wanted them to speak French all summer, so all the counselors and everybody there were French-speaking. They hired me because I was fairly fluent. I was the mother in one of the dorms and I ran the store for the camp. I thought it was a great place to be. I wasn't going to go home and loll around at my parents' house for the summer. I was going to do something interesting, and this was especially interesting to me.

I was put in a position of disciplining high-school girls who were fifteen and sixteen. The girls were supposed to have lights out at nine or ten o'clock, but they didn't want to go to bed. They wanted to sneak out and hang out with the boys in the neighboring camp. They wanted to talk half the night and would make quite a ruckus. I was only two years older than they were, and I was supposed to go in there and discipline these girls. It was absolutely impossible.

One night while these girls were carrying on, I sat on a

rock by the lake and called to God, "God, don't ever, in all my life, ever again put me in a position of responsibility over anybody or having to discipline anybody, because I don't want to do it. I don't want to have to tell people what to do. I don't want to have to face all this energy and all that I have to go through. Anything else I'll do, but don't make me have to discipline people."

This was one of my most fervent prayers before I became a messenger, before I even knew of that role. Looking back on this, I feel that this is the exact prayer that God has to hear before he will put someone in charge of others. For there is often an immense misuse of power that comes upon people when they desire power and they are put in positions of authority.

DURING CAMP WE had a weekend off. I got together with two of the other counselors at the camp who were French; they didn't speak much English at all. We decided to go hitchhiking to see Vermont and New Hampshire because none of us had ever seen them before.

I planned where we would go and I was aware of being guided. At every stop we would see whatever it was we had come to see. Then I would get the direction inside of me that a car was coming that would take us to the next place we had planned to go. So I would say, "Let's hurry up! We've got to get back to the road." As soon as we would get to the road, there would be the car. So I would stick out my thumb and it would stop, and I'd say, "We're going to so and so. Can we ride with you?" And the driver would say, "Yeah, I'm going there myself. Hop in."

That's what happened during the whole weekend. I

followed my inner guidance and it was absolutely correct. I
knew that it was inner guidance. I knew it was the divine
hand. I knew that I was in touch with what I would call God.
The biggest problem I had was keeping these two French girls
from dallying around.

I had my "I AM" books with me that summer. If I had an
hour off in the afternoon, I'd go hike somewhere in the woods
to read. I was reading those books the whole summer.

While I was at this summer camp, I wrote to the author of
The "I AM" Discourses, at the address in Chicago that was
listed in the book.

August 6, 1958

Dear Mr. King,

> For almost a year I have been reading *Unveiled
> Mysteries, The Magic Presence,* and *The "I AM"
> Discourses.* My understanding of God and his rela-
> tionship to man has been so clarified through this
> study that I can hesitate no longer to contact you, tell
> you of my joy in this newfound dominion and
> purpose.
>
> During the past ten years I have been an ardent
> student of Christian Science. I had already risen above
> much discord in my home and I had already chosen to
> serve God through the government in international
> relations when I stumbled upon your books on my
> mother's shelf, so I was well prepared to accept with-
> out question all that is revealed in them.
>
> As a student of Antioch College (Yellow Springs,
> Ohio) I was met with an avalanche of empirical,
> intellectual and moral temptations at the moment

when I was preparing to leave all to serve the Light. The past six months have been spent searching, pondering, examining. Before writing this letter I have again waited two months to be sure that what I am about to formally declare to you is not a passing whim.

It is with deep gratitude that I should like you to know, you who have given your life to this Great Service, that I, too, cherish the Inner Presence and the goal of Saint Germain on this continent. I am prepared to give unreservedly of myself to this cause. My life henceforth is entirely at the service of the Great Light.

I plan to earn a Bachelor of Arts in sociology or international relations and an interpreter's diploma from either the University of Munich or Geneva, and later on a Master's degree in a related field. Already this fall I shall have a position at the United Nations as part of Antioch's cooperative work-study program.

Since twenty years have lapsed since your books were first published, I am most interested to know if you and the students who first received the "I AM" Discourses are still in this sphere and what their various capacities are in our "Great Service."

If you would give me the addresses of any persons engaged in this activity in the vicinity of New York, Dayton or Mexico City, I shall be in each of these cities during the next eighteen months and would very much like to contact them. It would be a privilege to hear from you, Mr. King.

Sincerely yours,

Little did I know that Godfré Ray King was the pen name of Guy Ballard, that he had made his ascension the year I was born and that Mrs. Ballard was now the leader of their organization. The letter was returned to me marked "Unclaimed from Lock Box Section." I wrote a number of times without ever receiving a response.

Mark Prophet was in Washington, D.C., at this time, and it was on August 7, 1958, the day after I wrote this letter, that he, under El Morya's direction founded The Summit Lighthouse. And yet I did not meet Mark for a number of years afterwards and had no knowledge in my outer mind that this event was taking place.

Now I realize that this letter and the dedication and commitment it contains was my commitment to the inner calling to be a messenger, which I knew nothing about at the time. Many years later, El Morya told me that if I had not made this commitment and given this dedication to God, The Summit Lighthouse could not have been founded.

I am grateful that God inspired me to write this letter and that in my heart I was ready to write it, so there was no delay in the founding of The Summit Lighthouse. What this has taught me is that what we must do, we must do quickly. If we are prompted to act, then let us act. If an angel comes to us with direction, let us follow it immediately. Let us not think that God has forever or that we have forever.

26

The United Nations

IT SO HAPPENED that the camp counselor in the tent next to mine at École Champlain was the niece of the head of UNICEF. I told her that I was looking for a job and I wanted to work at the United Nations. I had the idea that I would study political science and work there. So she said, "Well, I'll call my aunt and I'm sure she can arrange an appointment for you to get where you want to go."

Soon afterwards, in the fall of 1958, after finishing my work at the camp, I was in New York City. I was going to interviews and trying to get a job at the United Nations, but a job was not forthcoming. I thought, "While I'm waiting for these various interviews, I'll go to the New York Public Library and I'll look up everything there is to be found on Saint Germain."

I took out all the cards on Saint Germain in the reference section and soon a librarian brought me about five stacks of books on this master, each about five feet high. You wouldn't believe the amount of information in the New York Public Library on Saint Germain, especially in accounts of the French

Revolution and European history. I thought I'd be there for a week!

As I sat down to look through this stack, I felt the master tap me on the shoulder. It wasn't a physical tap, but it was definitely the master, though he was not visible. He spoke to me and said to go back to the United Nations and go to the woman who was the head of UNICEF. He said that he had arranged for me to meet with her, and he would see to it that I got the proper job at the United Nations through her. And he said, "You'll have to hurry because she's about to leave, but I will hold her there until you arrive."

It seems that I took about eight steps and I was all the way out of the library, onto the street and into the first bus that was headed for the U.N. Grabbing the bus as it was leaving the curb, I felt like I was on wings. When I got to the U.N., I went to the desk and asked to see this woman. Her secretary returned the call and said that she was just leaving the office, but she would wait till I got there.

"Well, that's all in order," I thought. So I went up to her office and proceeded to tell her that I had met her niece when we were counseling in a summer camp together. She said that she would get me any job I wanted in the U.N. or in UNICEF, and she asked me what job I would like to have. Of course at UNICEF I'd be typing labels for Christmas cards that would be sent out all over the world, and I'd be stuck up on the ninth floor or the thirtieth floor somewhere.

I told her that I knew about the photographer down on the first floor, Leo Rosenthal, who photographed the delegates, that I would like to be his secretary and he had already interviewed me. So she recommended me to him and he gave me the job.

This job got me the contact I needed in order to

investigate and explore the U.N. from top to bottom. I had to be in all the committee meetings, I was back behind the scenes in the interpreters' booths, I got tickets to all of the banquets and gatherings, and I got to go to all of the embassies.

I met hundreds of delegates, ambassadors and representatives from all over the world every day since my job was to show them the latest pictures taken of them on the floor of the General Assembly, in the Security Council, in their private meetings, their receptions, and so forth. I had to know every one of these hundreds of people individually, memorize their names and faces, and match them with the photographs that I had in my files. And the moment one of them appeared at my desk, I had to look at the face, remember the name, pull his photographs and say, "Here you are, Mr. Ambassador. Here's this beautiful picture that you can send home and publish in your home newspaper." I was in a panic most of the time I worked there because I had to remember all these foreign names and faces, hundreds of them all descending upon me at once and demanding their pictures as they came out of their meetings.

During that experience, I learned that no matter who a person is, no matter what his great exalted position in the world is, no matter where he has come from, no matter what is behind him in wealth, power or position, the individual is still a man or a woman like me or anyone else. And I learned that the greatest men and women are the most humble, no matter where they are in government or in church. I learned that the people who are truly great and truly humble will deal with you on a one-to-one basis of equality, not of attainment but of opportunity. Here is a fellow man, a fellow woman, a soul with equal opportunity to make it in life.

There are those who do not have this attitude. They are

pompous, proud; they talk down their nose at you. They are demanding, commanding, ruthless, cruel. They are opportunists. And they make the little people, the children of God, feel that they are of no value, no worth and have no standing.

I had enough self-esteem in those days, enough awareness of the I AM Presence within me, that I knew who I was and I knew that no one there was better than I was. And I learned this by watching the behavior, sometimes extremely abominable, of these individuals. When I saw what was happening behind the scenes at the United Nations, immense corruption and sensuality, I knew for a certainty that God was not going to save the world through that organization.

I knew the place inside and out, and I knew that those people weren't solving the world's problems. I realized overwhelmingly that they were not idealists and did not have the welfare of the people at heart. I saw that they were engaged in a mad round of power politics and the manipulation of the economies. They were there for their egos, for how they looked back home, for politicking, and they didn't have the power of the Holy Spirit that it would take to bring about world peace. They were not working with the brotherhood of light, but they were on a quest for personal power. Their performance over the Hungarian uprising should have told me as much.

I HAD GONE to the U.N. with high ideals. I had grown up on the East Coast and my indoctrination was from the liberal establishment. I went to Eastern schools and learned political science the way it was taught in those schools. And I had every reason to believe that the U.N. was the hope of the world, because from the time we were little children through college this was what we had been told.

After my three-month co-op job at the United Nations, I came to realize that I knew everything I needed to know about it. I left there in December 1958, at the conclusion of the Thirteenth General Assembly, very disillusioned.

It was Saint Germain and not anyone in the physical who revealed to me that indeed the U.N. was not the hope of the world. This became a great crisis in my life. In fact, the awareness of what was really going on behind the scenes at the U.N. was so shocking to me that I was depressed for many months after I left, when I was back in Antioch doing my studies.

The United Nations left me with the realization that it would not be through the governments of the world that I could reach the people. In solving the world's problems, we would have to start back much further—within man, in his own concept of himself and his concept of God. God was the power, wisdom and love that would reveal the means to our victory in this age.

27

New York

WHILE I WAS in New York City, I went to an address I found in *The "I AM" Discourses*—the Gateway, East Sixtieth Street. I charged into the Gateway Bookstore and there was an older woman who looked quite mystical, as if she might be a student of the masters. I had an "I AM" book with me and told her I wanted to find more. I said, "You've got to tell me where I can find the Ballards. You've got to tell me where the 'I AM' Activity is."

But the woman said, "I'm not going to tell you, because if I tell you, you'll completely change your whole life for them." I couldn't get it out of her. I went back many times and she kept saying, "No, I'm not going to tell you." She sent me the books and I sent her checks for them, but she knew absolutely that she was not supposed to put me in touch with the "I AM" Activity.

One day I took five dollars worth of dimes and called every Ballard in the New York City phone book. Finally I decided that wasn't the way to find them. All those years I was looking for Saint Germain, the world was full of "I AM" students, and I didn't bump into one of them. It was like the angels were pulling them all out of the way.

DURING THE TIME that I was working at the United Nations, I took the opportunity one time when I was off work to go to the Indian Cultural Center and find out about teachings from the East. A tall, pretty Indian woman, wearing a sari, was in charge of the center. A yoga teacher was also there, so I decided to go to his classes to learn some yoga.

Soon after I started, I felt that the man who was teaching the class was developing an inordinate interest in me, beyond that which should exist between a teacher and a pupil. So I was feeling a little bit nervous about going to the center for instruction.

At the time I was living at home in Red Bank and commuting to the U.N. After about the second lesson, I found myself in my upstairs bedroom in my house in New Jersey and I felt this yoga teacher enter my forcefield, come into my mind and tell me to weigh myself and bring something to class the next time. When I got to class after that, he said, "Did you weigh yourself?" I looked at him and realized what he was doing, and it was the last time I ever went back.

I decided that this guy had his eye on me and did not have good intentions, and I was not going to have my mind manipulated by anyone. I didn't want any part of it. It was not of God; it was a psychic communication. Somehow he had developed his mental abilities and he was capable of doing this. I was not about to be associated with anyone who was going to violate my being in this way.

This was the last time I looked into yoga for some years. I was young and impressionable, and it was frightening to me.

28

Family Ties

GOD HAD BEEN the foundation of my life since I breathed my first breath, and long before. I endured a karmic circumstance that, I am convinced, was given to me for my learning and for my understanding of those who suffer under similar circumstances or worse.

Any time in my childhood that I was burdened, I would pray to Jesus to lead me to the scripture that would illumine me concerning the problem or challenge at hand. Without fail, I would open my Bible to a passage that would inspire me and give me the strength to carry on. I knew the presence of angels and was comfortable with ascended masters before I knew of their existence. In the middle of whatever else was going on around me, I determined to make my life a walk with Jesus. Sometimes when the turbulence was going on downstairs, I would retreat to my room, read my Bible and ask Jesus what was the meaning of the scriptures that I could not understand. And Jesus would instruct me.

My father and mother never talked about Jesus Christ as their Saviour. They never talked about being saved, never told me I needed to be saved and why.

Now I know why Saint Germain didn't make his presence known to me until after my graduation in 1957. It was because I first had to pass my tests and balance my karma in the Wulf family. And although I still had my human attachments and my psychology to deal with, at age eighteen I was cut free by Saint Germain, and I accepted my freedom.

I left home to get on with my mission, convinced that there was nothing I could do to stop the vicious self-destructive cycle perpetuated by both of my parents.

ALL THROUGH MY childhood, there had been a constant conflict in our home. It was almost a daily routine of alcohol, a fiery temper and a certain violence in the use of the voice. I was living under a great burden of fear.

As I grew older, I could not understand why my mother didn't just walk out and take me with her. On occasion she did, but each time she came back within a few days, and the fighting would start all over again. My mother always told me that she only stayed with my father because of me. So I took upon myself the burden that it was my fault that we had to go through these daily problems. My mother portrayed herself to me as the paragon of virtue, the one who was wronged and who was making all the sacrifices, and my father was the one doing all the yelling and causing all the problems.

When I was working at the U.N. and living at home in Red Bank, I told my mother, "I'm in college. I have a scholarship. There's no reason for you to stay here. You don't have to protect me; you're free. You can get a divorce." Without realizing it, I had called her bluff.

Finally she decided to go to Reno to divorce my father.

When he discovered that she had moved out, he figured I had something to do with it. So he was very angry at me, and he stood in the kitchen of our house and invoked the cursing of the devil upon me with the most intense energy I have ever seen. He cursed me with the full fury of his being, and until it was over I was literally frozen to that spot. I knew that a formal curse was being pronounced on me.

This was not the first time he had done such a thing. In moments of pride or pangs of conscience, my father told me of two occasions when he pronounced curses on people that had come to pass.

The first was against the man and his three sons who were my father's competitors in the boat business on the Shrewsbury River. They always wanted to buy him out, and they had approached him on several occasions to purchase his business. My father said to this man, "You will burn before I sell you my business," and he said this with the full intensity of his being. This was his way of saying, "Over my dead body."

My father was not a good businessman and didn't manage his funds well, and in the post-war downturn he was about to go bankrupt. These competitors were the only interested buyers, so he came to the place where he had to sell to them. But the night before the contract was to be signed, the father was smoking in bed and accidentally set the bed on fire. He burned to death.

The second occasion my father told me about was a similar case, where someone he saw as his enemy did something to him. He predicted to this man that he would drown, and he did.

I recognized my father's misuses of power. He knew how to pronounce a curse, and he was fully aware that he had a certain power in his cursing. I don't know where he learned this, whether it was in the Caribbean when he was there or just something he'd developed a momentum on over many lifetimes. In any case, when my father finished that curse against me, I walked out of the kitchen, went to the telephone at the Morrises' house and called Mrs. Schofield, my Christian Science practitioner. I told her what he had done, and she worked on it. I also did my own spiritual work on this with positive affirmations and what I knew from Christian Science and the "I AM" books.

So I moved out of the house and into an apartment in New York City to complete my co-op job. Because I spent all my salary on things like yoga, books and contributions to spiritual organizations, I never had much left for rent, so I didn't rent an expensive place. In fact, it was in quite poor surroundings near Columbia University.

After my mother's divorce was final, she came to New York City. I was full of joy and idealism, and it didn't make any difference to me what my surroundings were. But my mother thought my apartment was just terrible and she didn't want to stay there. I couldn't imagine that she would sell her soul for the price of simply going back to that house in Red Bank and having the security of a roof over her head. But within two days of arriving in New York, she did just that. She got on the bus, rode for an hour out of New York City, and went back home.

To me, it was like the Israelites wanting to go back to slavery in Egypt. My mother had friends and family all over the world whom she could have stayed with. Any number of people would have received her gladly. But she decided to go back to my father, though there was no earthly reason that she had to.

After I saw her off, I remember riding on the subway from my apartment, way up on the West Side, down to the U.N. on the East Side, and I felt more lonely than I had ever felt in all my life. I wept, because I was so completely and utterly disillusioned by the person in my life that I had held up as the image of motherhood.

I realized that my mother was not what she was telling me she was. She did not have the integrity to stand up against a very great darkness; and by being passive to it, she was the one who grounded this darkness in the earth. She provided the house and forcefield for my father to continue the darkness that he had sent forth all those years. I was idealistic at the time and I was not prepared to understand the frailties and imperfections of human nature. It was hard for me to face.

My mother went right back home to my father and moved in again. My father issued many ultimatums, including that she surrender ownership of property to him. He was extremely cruel, but she met all of his demands. They got married all over again, and the relationship continued as it always had. My mother's friend Agnes wrote me a comforting letter in which she said that my mother was a little flower that could not withstand transplanting.

I wept, too, for my mother, who had been conditioned so long to abuse as the only love she knew that she would rather return to that scene than face an unknown future. It was only then that I realized that I had not been the cause of her suffering nor of my father's tantrums. Perhaps I had been an excuse for the tantrums and the suffering to continue, but I had not been the underlying reason for them. My parents would rather be together in inharmony than apart from each other.

I HAD MADE my peace with my parents; now I must be at peace with myself. I was working with different material than they were, and the point of divergence was my spiritual path.

I can remember that as a teenager I had to distinguish between the will of my parents and the will of God in my life. When I began to travel or go to summer camp at age fourteen and fifteen and later when I went abroad to study, my parents, like any other parents, had to adjust to my becoming an adult. I remember on one or two occasions getting the strong compulsion that for some reason I should go home and then traveling a great distance to be there, only to find that this was not a calling from God. It was my parents indulging in their own self-pity that I was not there and willing me back by their own self-will. I had great love and respect for my parents, but at those moments I knew that I was supposed to be somewhere else.

When I entered the house and I felt this vibration and saw this energy, I had a deep lesson on interpreting forcefields— interpreting the things that pull upon me and defining what was someone else's mind and what was my own. I learned that when you think you want to do something and the desire is so powerful that you think it must be right, it may be someone else's mind and will deciding what they want you to do, and their mind is more powerful than yours at that moment. So I found that I had to know my own will and my own determination of what I was going to do in life. And I had to stick with it, no matter what might be the wind and the gale that was coming against my ship.

MOST CHILDREN DON'T deal with returning karma until puberty, but some do ask God, before they come into embodiment, if they can begin balancing their karma from conception on. After I had been through my first eighteen years and learned the meaning of karma and the choices I had made before birth, including being born to the specific parents I had, I saw in the akashic records that I had chosen to deal with my karma immediately. Thus I am aware that all whom I met during my childhood and teenage years were integral to the process of my sowing and reaping both the positive and negative karma that I had incurred in previous lifetimes.

God blessed me with caring parents who did the best they could with what they had to offer. They had led full and interesting lives before meeting and marrying, and they brought with them the traditions of Europe and the lands of their birth, Germany and Switzerland. I felt that I had a rich heritage and I understood my roots. People are not perfect and we shouldn't expect them to be, so I count as a blessing my opportunity to learn the lessons of life from the father and mother God gave to me.

I know that God brought me to this family to be a comforter, to love both of my parents through their trials, and to experience whatever karma I myself had in the midst of their karma. I am grateful, oh so grateful to God, for these experiences, even though they were a burden. For I learned to identify the good and evil forces that alternately occupy the bodies of men, women and children, that I might be the instrument of God's healing to them, according to his will.

I learned true compassion that does not sympathize with anyone's demons but calls on the two-edged sword of the Holy Spirit to separate a man from his demons and then to bind those demons so that they invade not another empty house. Finally I learned how all-encompassing is the merciful heart of the Divine Mother. Because she could forgive, I could forgive, knowing that God would repay, for justice belongs to him. And the quality of mercy held in my heart must be a fount of transmutation dissolving the cause, effect, record and memory of what appears so real but in divine reality is not.

Mary Baker Eddy reawakened my understanding of this great truth, but my soul knew it well. "Evil is not real and its appearance has no power!" as Charles M. Carr, my beloved Christian Science teacher of later years, used to say.

I only regret that I could not help my parents find healing, the same healing that I had found since my earliest communion with my heavenly Father and Mother, with Jesus, the saints, the angels and the nature spirits.

The night my father fell asleep to the sleep of the ages, he wrestled in his bed with the death angel who had come to take him. By that time it was too late for my mother to start a new life, but fifty years of her own pent-up anger began to show itself in all directions. She died five months after my father, never having found peace, never knowing God as her divine deliverer, still in fear of death and what lay beyond.

Oh, how I loved you, my father and my mother. Oh, how I loved you. Would to God that my love could have made the difference.

29

"Go to Boston!"

I HAD A friend at Antioch whose name was Bob Bachman. He was a devout Catholic and he was fond of me in the sense that he was my protector, because I was one of the few girls on campus who had any religion. He was very kind to me and helped me pack up and go back to Antioch after my three months working at the U.N.

One day I confided to him that I was looking for Saint Germain. He said, "Betty, you're never going to find Saint Germain on this campus." And I said to myself, "He's absolutely right. I'm never going to find Saint Germain out here." No truer words were ever spoken. So I prayed, and the voice of God said, "Go to Boston!"

I WENT BACK to Antioch for winter quarter 1959 and then spent spring quarter at Tufts University in a co-op job as a secretary in the Department of Applied Experimental Psychology, where I typed reports on animal experimentation. I picked the job because I wanted to go to Boston, and Tufts

University was outside of Boston. I transferred to Boston University in the fall.

While I was working at Tufts, I also took a psychology course. I wanted to get into a situation where I could see psychology used as a therapy. So I decided I would use my evenings to work at a private hospital for alcoholics. I wasn't going to be paid. I just volunteered, and they said, "Sure, come over."

So several evenings each week, after I finished my day's work, I would get on the subway and go off to this hospital. They assigned me to talk to people that were in there for rehabilitation.

I learned a lot about alcoholics while I was there. Their families brought them to the hospital when they were totally drunk. Night after night after night, they would tell me why they were alcoholics. And it was always about what everybody else had done to them. They didn't own themselves. They could not own up to their own being, their own actions.

They would go through the process of getting off the alcohol and then getting on a good diet and having some kind of therapy. Then they would be sent home. And in six weeks or six months, the drinking would begin all over again. It was very repetitive. And so I saw the challenge: How do you instill a sense of self-determination into people when the will is lacking?

This was an amazing experience for me, because I never realized the way alcoholics think, what makes them tick and what is their psychology. I had a wonderful time volunteering at this hospital and I felt that I brought some joy and comfort to the people there. It was a stepping-stone in my life.

WHILE I WAS at Tufts, I met someone who was to have a great influence on me. Back in high school, a friend's mother had told me about a Christian Science practitioner by the name of Charles M. Carr. She had gone to him for migraine headaches and he had healed her. But all she could talk about was how much money he had charged her. I thought that the woman was truly ridiculous to be worrying about what she had paid for a healing when she had been in lifelong misery from these headaches. And I said to myself, "I want to meet this Christian Science practitioner who can heal somebody of their migraine headaches."

So I had it in my mind that I would go meet him one day. On one of my trips back home to New Jersey, I went to see him in his office on Fifth Avenue in New York.

I'm not sure of his age. He appeared to be in his forties or fifties, but it could have been that his gray hair made him look older than he was. He welcomed me into his office and we had a heart-to-heart talk. I don't know how long it was, but instantaneously we both felt a strong bonding.

While I was in his office, a light of God came down upon me and I could feel it tangibly. I had never felt such a light in my life and I knew that he had been the instrument of it. This was the first person I had ever met in whose presence I felt such a stupendous light descend to me from God. I had certainly felt light and love in the presence of Mrs. Schofield, but this was something else. This was more powerful. All I wanted to do was to be able to keep that light.

After I left his office, I took a train and some rowdy guys were riding in the same carriage. They were being obnoxious, and I could feel them and the energy they were throwing at me, and it felt as if they were peeling the light away from me. I didn't know how to keep this light, and I could see that it was dissipating because I was out in the world in this unfortunate situation.

So that summer, in August 1959, I applied to Mr. Carr and he accepted me into his class. In Christian Science, selecting a teacher is an important process. According to Mrs. Eddy's *Manual of the Mother Church,* a teacher is allowed thirty students per year. He teaches a class for two weeks, and those students remain his for the rest of their lives, consulting him and looking to him for guidance.

Many people in the church were already calling me and asking me to pray for their healing, because they found out that when I prayed for them they got well. So my goal was to become a Christian Science practitioner. All my life I had been pointed in that direction.

The way I found my mission in life was that I would do the closest thing to it that I could conceive of at the time. I didn't know what I was moving toward, but every day of my life I was trying to approximate the very best thing I could do in the service of God.

30

Inner Work

DURING MY STUDENT days at Boston University, I felt in my soul and in my being a great love for God. And I felt that the teachings I understood at that time, which I had derived solely from Christian Science and the "I AM" books, made me a human misfit in terms of any man ever wanting to marry me. So I was resigned that I would not be married, since I knew of no one who could accept a wife who had such beliefs and such firm convictions.

One day, as I had done all of my childhood, I picked up the Bible to seek a response from God to these thoughts. I opened to chapter 54 of the Book of Isaiah, which said: "For thy Maker is thine husband; the LORD of hosts is his name; and thy Redeemer the Holy One of Israel; the God of the whole earth shall he be called."

I realized that this was the most important marriage of my whole life, to be married to God. I knew the I AM Presence, the Presence of God with me, and I said to myself, "Surely if I can become acceptable in the sight of God as the least of his brides, I should be on the way to finding Saint Germain."

I found this period in my life to be one of profound meditation and communion.

WHILE I WAS living in Boston and attending Boston University, I became quite involved in the Christian Science church. I was an usher in the Mother Church, taught Sunday school there, and worked for the *Christian Science Monitor*. For a few weeks, during another secretary's absence, I was also the secretary to Erwin Canham, who was the editor then. Following that, I worked in the Department of Branches and Practitioners, and I became the president of the Christian Science students organization at Boston University.

From all these experiences, I learned a great deal about the publishing operations of a church and also about the organization and administration of a church on a worldwide scale. All that I saw, heard, witnessed and participated in, every single detail, has helped me to see how our church should be organized today.

During the time I was in Boston, when I was twenty to twenty-two years old, I applied the principles of Christian Science healing on behalf of anyone in the church who would ask me for my prayerful support. Friends reported to me that they were being healed. But I also saw that rather than doing their own work, they began to depend on me to do it for them. I thought to myself that it was more important for them to strengthen themselves in the practice of Christian Science than to depend on me or anyone else to do it for them.

The healings that were taking place in those instances were largely a testimony to my progress on the path and not to theirs. In my heart I knew that spiritual progress was more important than physical healing. And in all cases, physical healing must be the outward sign of the soul's advancing footsteps. Then and there I saw that I must comfort by teaching as well as by healing, for without understanding there can be no permanent healing.

ONE MORNING ON my way to work at the *Christian Science Monitor*, I had a remarkable experience. I was supposed to be there at five A.M. to deliver the stories that had come in overnight to the desks of all the reporters. I got up early and was walking to my job. I liked to walk, even though it was a number of miles, because I enjoyed the dawn and the morning.

This particular morning, at that early hour, there was hardly anyone out at all, no one on the streets and not many cars. All of a sudden, I experienced being very high above myself, looking down at myself walking to work. It seemed as if I was hundreds of feet above my body, watching this little person that was me going to work.

At the same time, as I looked down at myself, I saw that lower self as mortal. And I saw that I was one in my I AM Presence, looking down upon me. God allowed me to see my immortality, to realize what part of me was walking, the lesser part of me, and to know that the greater part of me was already in heaven. And I knew that I had to stay with that body and that soul until all of my being would become one integrated personality in God.

WHEN I WAS looking for the master Saint Germain in Boston, I was trying to figure out why I wasn't meeting him. Eventually I came to the realization that it all depended on me and that what was inside of me was determining my fate. I believed strongly that whatever came into my life—people, conditions or circumstances—was a mirror of something in my own inner consciousness I needed to deal with. If I attracted good, I might know that some good of God was in me. And if I attracted those things that were not the best, I might certainly explore my inner self to see what I might find.

I remember the day I moved into the first apartment I had while I was in college. I couldn't afford much and it was something I had to take in desperation. As I looked around me, I saw that it certainly was not the surroundings I was accustomed to. In fact, it was on the verge of being squalor. It was a basement apartment and the vibrations were terrible—an oppressive feeling, with the heaviness and weight of the city.

So I communed with God and said, "Dear God, I know that if I am here, it's because I have work to do here. There is something in me that has attracted this place to me. I know that God is here and God is in me, and he will not leave my soul to suffer in hell." So all day I gave gratitude for God and his presence.

It gave me a great sense of joy to commune with God in this manner. I sensed the challenge and I totally accepted the responsibility for being in this place, and I accepted that it reflected some lack in my own consciousness.

After I got through saying this, I was completely happy. For I knew I was living in the aura of God. I rejoiced in the opportunity I was being given and I felt the promise of life. It really didn't matter where I was.

I went about my business and I made this little basement apartment as beautiful as I could with whatever I had. And I determined that I would stay in this apartment until I had learned the lesson I needed to learn from being there and gain my victory.

Within two weeks someone offered me a beautiful apartment on the top floor of a place with lots of sunshine and bay windows. I happily moved in, painted the whole apartment myself, got some second-hand furniture, and made a cheerful little home. I was grateful for the lesson of this experience because I knew that my circumstances were the product of my own limitations.

A little while later, just at the moment I was probably carrying this concept a little bit too far, I was sitting on the bus riding by the Boston Common. I looked out the window and saw what to me was the most loathsome of all beasts. Right there, walking along the Boston Common, at the end of a leash that was being towed by a woman, was an anteater!

To me, there was nothing more repulsive in this world than an anteater. I looked out the window, I saw this thing, and I thought to myself, "Ye gods, what is wrong with you? Why are you seeing this anteater?"

So I decided that I had some work to do, that this anteater must be bringing me a message. And I also looked around at the people I was associating with, and I realized that they were also products of my state of consciousness. There was something I must do with my consciousness to be ready for Saint Germain.

31

"Obey Immediately"

AS A CHILD I had a stern father who exacted obedience at the snap of a finger. This was understood in our household. I wondered at times why I had such a strict father. But when I met El Morya and realized that his forte and his way of training disciples was discipline and obedience to the will of God, I understood that he put me in that house for a good reason.

As I have mentioned, when I left home and went to college, I was looking for Saint Germain, but he didn't appear to me and I couldn't see him. So I thought I must not be ready for my service to him and I wondered, "How shall I get ready?" Then I thought to myself, "I must obey immediately every word of God that comes into my soul."

While I was a student at Boston University, I wrote on the brown paper covers of my textbooks "Obey Immediately." So I couldn't look at a textbook without being reminded that that's what I needed to do. Even as I walked to my classes, I would see those words on my books. I was always listening to God because one of these days God was going to tell me where Saint Germain was and I had to be ready.

So that was my self-discipline. I would meditate within and listen for God. I would listen with a keen ear, as one would try to hear the call of a distant bird or a sound that was soundless. I know now that I was making the transition from the outer ear to the inner ear, a transition we all must make in order to hear the voice of God.

God spoke to me and told me many things and taught me many things. And when I received the word to do something specific—to render a service for someone, to go somewhere or to give a fiat—I would always remember that even if it was a sacrifice, it must be done quickly, immediately. For I knew that I would miss the next cycle or the next opportunity on the ladder of initiation if I did not obey the first step, because all is timing in the great eternal Now.

One day I had an interesting experience. The net result was a total shock to my consciousness and then a long period of deep meditation and communion within on many concepts I derived from the event.

That particular day I was in my dormitory, an old town-house on Beacon Street, which was at least five or six blocks from school. When I got up in the morning, I checked to see what the weather was and what I should wear. It was early spring in New England, when the weather was often temperamental and cold. But this day it was amazingly warm. It was like a mild spring day, even though it was late February or early March.

So I thought, "All I need to wear is a sweater." But the voice of God spoke to me loudly and clearly and said, "Put on your coat that is fur-lined, your fur hat and your mittens." It was almost like my conscience was speaking. Before I even realized what that voice was, I thought, "That's the most ridiculous thing I've ever heard," and I put my arm out the window again to be sure I wasn't feeling the heat from the radiator.

The birds were chirping, the buds on the trees were beginning to come out and it seemed like a warm spring day. But the voice was definitely clear and distinct. So I said, "All right, I'll put on the fur-lined coat, but I'm not going to wear mittens and I'm not going to wear a hat," and I trotted off to school with my books.

When I got to the last block before school, I decided I might be late for class, so I started to run. As the traffic was stopped for a red light, I went charging diagonally across the street and ran straight into a person on a bicycle that was going at high speed. It was a head-on collision and I was thrown down on the ground on my hands. My body was completely protected by my fur coat. But where I had braced myself with my hands, I had gotten scratched up and I was bleeding.

I wasn't hurt, but I was amazed at the exact direction of the voice of God. And I was amazed to realize that if I had been completely obedient, I would have been fully protected.

I got up and went to class, and I was profoundly moved. Not only did I realize that God knew that this was going to happen and I had disobeyed his voice, but there was a certain element of predestination in it. God knew beforehand that I was going to get to that place, I was going to run, there was going to be a bike there, and I was going to crash into it.

And I thought, "How can this be? Is everything in our life preplanned like this? Can you know to the exact day and hour that something will happen? Does God have it all on a chart up there? What's going on?"

I thought that all this was a great marvel. It was a mystery to me.

"Obey Immediately"

MY DORM MOTHER was a devout Catholic, and she understood that I couldn't stay in that dorm with the usual things that go on in dorms, so she would let me go out at night. I just had to go out and walk and talk to God, and I would always talk to him about his mysteries. I had to discover what these mysteries were.

An understanding of reincarnation and karma showed to me that life is not predestined. It's based on free will. We have set up our karma by our use of free will in the past, and that karma comes due with exact, mathematical, geometric precision. So because of our past freewill choices, it can be calculated that we are going to meet certain obstacles on certain days, and we're going to bump into ourselves and our karma.

After that incident with the bike, from that day on wherever I walked, whatever I did, I was listening. I asked God to forgive me, and I promised that I would obey his voice, whatever he told me to do. And so I developed an inner listening, because I knew I would never find Saint Germain if I was not obedient to this voice. And I became much more diligent thereafter in practicing obedience.

These lessons continued, and I ceased to rely on my logic, but I relied only on my attunement and the voice of God that spoke to me. I did exactly what I was told to do. And I found that I grew spiritually, and a great deal of grace and spiritual wisdom was imparted to me. As this wisdom began to dawn in my consciousness, I was aware of how ignorant I was. For when we contact the wisdom of God, we cannot help but realize what poor moths we are, dancing around the flame, and how little we have. We are but a lump of clay.

Since the stream of wisdom was flowing to me, I decided it would be well to pray to God to give me greater wisdom. So I developed a habit of walking many hours a day alone in areas that were quiet and asking God to illumine me. My prayer was, "I know nothing. I need to know more to help mankind. Please illumine me." This went on for some time. Later I realized that my obedience to God in understanding that I must ask for wisdom in order to receive it led me also to the feet of the masters.

32

Marriage

WHILE I WAS in Boston, I met a young man about five years older than I was. He was a law student and a leader in the youth fellowship at the Mother Church. His name was Dag Ytreberg and he was part Norwegian and part Swedish. The first time I saw him, a block away, I recognized him; he also recognized me.

I knew him, but I did not know him with the stunning impact of love at first sight. I kept on seeing him and I kept on saying to myself, "I know this person. I know this person."

So I joined the youth group, and we started talking and got to know each other. We found out that we had things in common—my parents were European, like his; I majored in political science and he was interested in international relations.

We would go here and there together, and I kept feeling that I was being drawn to him by a camaraderie and an attraction. In retrospect I realize that it was an energy which was not a love sufficient and necessary to warrant a lifetime commitment, but one that mandated itself in our lives until the cycles would run their course. Evidently, our souls needed each other, and there was something we had to give to one another.

Once early in the relationship, I found out that he was sick. And God said to me, "Go and take him some food." So I went to his apartment and I brought him some food, which was an act of service. I was serving his life. The necessity of the law of karma was fulfilling itself. He also, as well as his mother and brother, went out of his way to express kindness to me in little and larger ways. By and by, we became closer and closer friends, and he asked me to marry him.

So I said to him, "Well, you see, there is one complication. I'm looking for the master Saint Germain, and here's his picture. When I find him, I'm going to serve him wherever he calls me. So if we get married, you have to realize that I've been looking for him for years; and the day he comes, that will be it. He's going to be the center of my life."

At the time I was a dedicated Christian Scientist and so was he. He never thought I would actually come to the point where I would say, "OK, here we go. I'm going to follow Saint Germain." Nor did I realize that when Saint Germain came, my whole life would be turned upside down. And in order to serve him, I would walk out of the Mother Church forever and never look back. So he was agreeable to my terms because he read into them the consistency of my lifestyle and character. I think that the events which were to come to pass were far beyond the scope of our ability to foresee.

I also said, "Well, you have to meet Mr. Carr, and if Mr. Carr doesn't approve of this marriage, then I'm not going to get married." So Dag was nervous about meeting him. But as it happened, they got along famously. Mr. Carr put him at ease and said he thought we'd make a great match. So did

Mrs. Schofield. In fact, part of my decision to marry him was based on their telling me to get married. I really listened to Mrs. Schofield, and she advised me to marry him. She said, "Oh, take it, Betty. Take it, Betty."

So we decided to plight our troth. And for some impelling reason that I could not explain, I did marry him. I just had the sense and the direction that I should do so. I was determined that until and unless I was obedient to every direction God gave me, I would not find Saint Germain, and I knew that one step would lead to the next. I knew that when I was ready, if I was truly ready, Saint Germain would come and get me and show me what he wanted me to do. And if marrying this man was part of that path, then I would gladly do it.

We went home to New Jersey to my parents' house and we were married in a little country church in Shrewsbury. It was a hometown wedding with all the old friends and neighbors. Since we were on a students' budget, I borrowed a nice little organdy wedding dress from my Greek neighbor. After we said our vows before the altar, we came walking down the aisle. We were in the newness of life's adventure, with the hope for the future to write upon the clean white page the story of love. Then suddenly, without warning, the Holy Spirit spoke to me loud and clear. And to my astonishment, I heard the words: "It is but for a little while."

I looked up as if it had been part of a running conversation of my soul with the eternal Spirit at inner levels. Without missing a step, I responded, as faces smiled and beamed on both sides of the aisle, "All right." And out the door we went to greet our guests in the receiving line. To my dismay, though it was played I never heard the "Triumphal March" from *Aïda*, which I had requested. It would have to wait for another day and for the real triumph of my soul through this karmic marriage and beyond.

After the reception we drove back to Boston, moved into a basement apartment and continued with school. I still hadn't found Saint Germain but I kept on looking. At the time I was working and Dag was going to law school. My desire was to help him in every way, but I could not give up my own education and career, as some well-meaning advisers thought I should, for the sake of the marriage.

It was not a perfect relationship. We never became as one person, as I have come to realize it is possible to do. We were also young and a bit immature at the time—a little self-willed, each protective of his own identity, not as capable of self-giving as each of us would be in later years. Even his mother, whom I dearly loved, confided in me later that we didn't love each other enough for the marriage to last.

ONE DAY I was in our apartment and I was having a difficult time. Dag was sick, and I could feel a burden upon me and a weight of circumstances and people. So I said this prayer: "God, if you will just give to me now a greater vision of your church, this Mother Church, I know that I'll have the inspiration to go on."

Then I walked the two blocks down the street to the Mother Church. I went up to one of the main doors as I thought to myself, "Just let me touch this church." So I put my hands on the outside wall near the side of the door. As I did so, I looked up and saw a huge angel standing there, a giant fiery-white seraphim. There was one on each side of the door.

I had never seen an angel look so physical. God had opened my sight, and I thought, "Can this be?"

It was hard to deal with. How do you react and what do you do, now that you've seen these angels? I ran around the whole block to every single door of the church. At every door, two angels were standing guard.

After I had touched the church wall and seen those angels, I went home. I put my hands on Dag and he was instantly healed. To me, this was a confirmation of the reality of those angels and their power.

I knew that angels were real and that they were sent by God to communicate with us and to help us. But my teachers in Christian Science were not willing to let me believe this. Although Mary Baker Eddy taught about angels as being real beings, her statement affirming this is ignored, and the standard interpretation in Christian Science is that angels are "God's thoughts passing to man."[49] In other words, angels are just ideas.

Christian Scientists believe that Mary Baker Eddy's word is infallible and that she gave the complete and final revelation of truth. It's hard to walk away from a belief system like that.

SOON AFTERWARDS, I had another profound experience. It happened one day when I was ushering in church. Because Christian Scientists have a metaphysical belief system, they do not have ornate sanctuaries. There are no pictures, no statues, no symbols. What replaces all of this are sayings of Jesus carved or imprinted on the wall. The Mother Church in Boston is large, so it has many walls and many writings carved into those walls.

So I was standing at the back of the church and Jesus prompted me to turn around. When I did, I looked at the wall and saw these words inscribed there in gold: "Other sheep I have, which are not of this fold: them also I must bring, and they shall hear my voice; and there shall be one fold, and one shepherd."[50]

It was as if I had never heard that phrase before. Jesus was there and I was electrified by his presence. He was calling me. And I understood that I must leave this church, that he had another fold. He was calling me to go out and find his other sheep, those who were not within the context of this movement or any movement of Christianity. He was saying, "This is not your fold; this is not the place of your preaching or your mission." And he was referring to the mission for which he had prepared me.

I had to go and find the sheep that Jesus was going to bring—those who would hear the voice of the ascended master Jesus Christ as I had heard him speaking to me in my heart all of my life, those who would let go of all moorings to follow only him all the way back to the Father on the path of the ascension.

Who were they? Where were they? And how would I find them? These questions I pondered as I stood before that wall and felt that call.

I was twenty-two. I was ready for the next step. But I still had to find the staircase.

33

"I Can't Wait Any Longer!"

DURING MY SECOND year in Boston, I was working as a secretary for the president of a small insurance company, and I would spend my lunch hours trying to find Saint Germain. As part of my quest, I went to every secondhand bookstore I could find. I thought that if I could find some place where the books were sold, I could find the Ballards, and then I could find Saint Germain.

One day I went into a bookstore and they had the books. So I said to the owner, "Does anyone ever come in here and buy these books?" And he said, "Yes, there is one man, a doctor, and he comes in every so often and he buys up every book we have."

Then I said, "I have to find this doctor." But the bookstore owner didn't know his name. So I said, "The next time he comes in, will you please get his name and phone number so I can contact him."

Every day I would go back and see if he had come in. All I needed to do was to stand at the door and the owner would look at me and shake his head and I would go on my way.

Well, that method never proved to be the one that worked. I never did find this doctor through this means.

MEANWHILE, MY MOTHER had a close friend from Asbury Park whose name was Paula Grable. While I was away at school, my mother lent this woman one of my "I AM" books. When I found out, I said, "Mother, I can't believe you let go of one of my 'I AM' books and lent it without my permission. Get that book back from her or I might never see it again. I have to have that book."

Paula read the book and decided that she would go to New York to find the contact of the "I AM" Activity, because I had never been able to find it. So she went to New York, and while she was there she had an appointment with a hairdresser she used to see there. As Paula was having her hair done, the hairdresser asked her what she was doing in New York. Paula thought to herself, "What would you know about the ascended masters' teachings?" So she wasn't going to bring up the subject. But by and by as the conversation went on, she finally decided to tell the hairdresser that she was in New York to find Saint Germain, the "I AM" Activity and anybody who knew about those teachings.

It so happened that the hairdresser was a member of the Bridge to Freedom, which was another organization sponsored by the ascended masters. So through Paula Grable I was put in touch with the Bridge to Freedom, the first ascended master organization I was ever in contact with. I wrote to them and they wrote back.

I learned that there was an ascended master sanctuary in New York City that was associated with the Bridge to Freedom and they invited me to visit. I was so excited about this. When the end of the week came and I finished work, I hopped on a train from Boston to New York.

The head of that center was a strong woman of about sixty-five or seventy. I told her that I had been a Christian Scientist and had studied the "I AM" books. So she sat me down and said to me, "Matter is real! Mary Baker Eddy is wrong! Matter is real!" And she said a number of other things which she cited in the teachings of Mary Baker Eddy that she said were not true.

Since I was nine, I had believed, as I had been taught, that matter is not real.[51] So it was quite a shocking experience to be told this, and I remember distinctly in my heart how I gulped. I closed my eyes and it was almost like my internal being was shaking; I could feel in my being an involuntary trembling. It was not that I had fear but that something at a subconscious level, at the very foundation of my being, a pillar of a religious tenet, was being shaken when I was told that it was incorrect.

In order to get through that day, I had to have absolute trust in God and in the ascended masters. I said in my heart, "This must be a very key test, so I am going to set aside my religious beliefs and accept what this woman is telling me and see where it leads me." I spoke to God and I surrendered the whole teaching of Christian Science. If my entire lifetime of studies was of something that was not correct, then I was willing to surrender it. I don't know why I had the courage to do this; I have seldom seen other people who could.

That was my first test. The second test was that she took an entire hour to tell me about this awful, awful man in Washington, D.C., who claimed to be a messenger. I had not yet heard of Mark Prophet and I had no idea who she was talking about. With her European accent, she talked on and on, and I could not understand why she was carrying on about this terrible man. Why wasn't she telling me about the teachings of the ascended masters?

But her conversation went in one ear and out the other, and I think that it was the blessing of my Christ Self that it was just meaningless to me. And even when Mark Prophet came to Boston, I'm not sure I made the connection that this was who she had been talking about.

While I was at that center, I walked around the sanctuary, looked at the pictures and meditated upon the masters. I was in seventh heaven. For the first time, I saw El Morya's picture, and I saw pictures of other masters. At long last, after years of searching, I was finally in a sanctuary dedicated to the ascended masters.

I learned that meetings were being held in downtown Boston on the second or third floor in a building off Commonwealth Avenue. This was a building I went by every day on my way to Boston University from my apartment on St. Stephen Street. Every single time I had walked past this building, a voice had said to me, "Go inside and see what's in there." But I would answer the voice and say, "I'm late for class. I can't go in right now." So I never did go in.

And so it was through the Bridge to Freedom that I found this activity in Boston. The head of it was the doctor, the very one who used to go to that secondhand bookstore. His name was Dr. Whitney and by that time he was an elderly man. I wasn't intended to come into the knowledge of the ascended masters' activity through the Bridge to Freedom. But that is how God worked, by grace, to save me from my not following that inner direction.

ONCE I MADE contact with Dr. Whitney, I would never leave him alone. His office was between my apartment and Boston University. I would stop there on my way to and from class and wait in his waiting room. When all the other patients were done, he would take me in and I would ask him questions, questions, questions, and he would answer all of them patiently until I had no more. Then I would go home and read the teachings of the masters, and I would come back the next day, wait in the waiting room and ask more questions. Sometimes I would have to wait an hour or two until the patients were through before I could ask him more questions.

Mr. Whitney was a lovely person. He had a small room where he held his meetings. At each meeting and each decree session, he would bank the entire altar with fresh flowers, and the whole room would have a wonderful fragrance.

He had many friends who were part of the group, some of them quite elderly. In order to fill his meetings, he would have to go out in his car and drive from house to house around the city to collect all these dear people, chauffeur them to the meeting, escort them up and sit them down. And when the meeting was over, he would chauffeur them all home again, which he gladly did in order to have a meeting.

I attended services at Dr. Whitney's while working at the Mother Church, being married and going to school.

IN APRIL 1961, I was reading in the newspaper about events in Cuba and the Caribbean. It was a key turning point, and I could see the possibility of Communism spreading through the whole hemisphere. I wept and wept and wept when I read the newspaper. It was the most terrible day of my life. There I was, weeping, and Dag came home. And in the tradition of

203

Christian Science, he said, "What are you crying about? It's not real."

People in Christian Science circles tend to think that just about everything is not real. Error is not real. Matter is not real. Nothing that's unpleasant is real. And they cease to deal realistically with life. That's not the way Mary Baker Eddy was, but that is how some of her followers have become.

So there he was. That was as much accountability as he was going to take for the world scene. I was taking responsibility; the Caribbean was my problem. What was I going to do about it? That's how I looked at it. I knew that Saint Germain had the answers.

I was desperate. I could feel the decades turning and I could feel that there was imminent danger. I felt that finding Saint Germain was going to be the key to understanding the new age that was dawning upon us. And yet I wasn't any nearer to finding him or his teaching.

So I leaped from my seat and ran up a couple of flights of stairs to the roof of my apartment. I threw my arms up into the blue sky and the billowing clouds, and I cried into that sky, "Saint Germain, I know you're up there! You've got to come and get me now! I can't wait any longer!"

I was demanding and I was fearless. And I felt the light and love go out from me, and I felt it reach its mark. I knew he was there, and I was at peace.

Less than a week after making that fiat, I received a phone call from Dr. Whitney telling me that the messenger Mark Prophet would be in town that evening and he would deliver a lecture and a dictation. I was thrilled! I had to be there and I had to meet this messenger. After all of these years trying to find Godfré Ray King, to no avail, I had to hear a dictation.

I literally ran to this meeting. I was so excited and I

wanted to be on time. My heart was pounding. I just couldn't believe it. I was finally going to meet the messenger of the ascended masters.

34

Mark Prophet

IT WAS APRIL 22, 1961. I sat down in that tiny little room in that old building in Boston. Just a handful of people were there. When I sat down, I found myself sitting opposite the messenger Mark Prophet.

I looked into his eyes and I realized then that I had been looking for that pair of eyes all of my life. I can only describe them as a pair of eyes that had met the eyes of God. He had a profound understanding, a wisdom and a love that was extraordinary. I knew that I had found the one who could open the door of consciousness. I had found my teacher.

Having glimpsed the reality that shone forth from him, I closed my eyes and began to meditate. While I was meditating, I noticed a tremendous power. It was his aura. I was feeling an energy and a forcefield that I had never felt before. I had met many people so far in my life—traveling overseas; going to college for four years; working for the Mother Church and the *Christian Science Monitor,* at an insurance company, at the U.N.; moving among the rich and powerful. I had studied Eastern teachings. But in all my wanderings,

I hadn't found one person whose aura enveloped me with such an energy, the same intense power I had known as a child as the power of the Holy Spirit.

In the course of meditating, I found myself being drawn up into the "mantle" of a prophet. This mantle is a symbol of an individual's light, or attainment, like the robe of Christ or the mantle of Elijah that fell on Elisha. And that's just what it felt like. I was being swept up into the garment of his soul. It was a spiral that was taking me to another plane of con-sciousness—until I found myself standing with Mark Prophet, looking into galaxies of light, being shown how science and religion are one, how there is a fiery core, a permanent atom, a Great Central Sun, which we've never even glimpsed from this point in cosmos, and galaxies of light revolving around it. I could see energy moving. I could see energy as a rotation of being, of the polarity of God, masculine and feminine.

He showed me how energy as a principle becomes per-sonified in the manifestation of individuality at all different levels of being—Elohim, archangels, seraphim, cherubim, solar hierarchies and, finally, closer to earth, ascended masters. These masters are people like you and me who were simply a little bit brighter, a little bit more illumined. They had transcended this plane and had overcome the problem of disease and death.

Finally he showed me with his hand a group of souls just like myself. They were the group that I had come from, and they had not yet resolved the problem of being; they had not yet transcended this plane. They were scheduled to take embodiment East and West in all religions and cultures. They had one thing in common—they knew who they were, where they had come from and where they had lived before. They understood the sine wave of our evolutions in Spirit and

Matter planes, in and out of the mansions of God. They understood cosmic law. They understood energy and they knew why they were embodying—to keep a flame of freedom at all levels of human endeavor.

Then Mark turned and showed me another group of souls. They were already in embodiment, and they appeared on the screen of consciousness like little candle flames. They were here and there and everywhere, in all of the nations and religions of the world. When I looked at these souls, I recognized them as my brothers and sisters. I knew them right away.

Then he drew me in, giving me a close-up reading of their auras and their minds and what they were thinking, and he showed me something that was the most startling revelation. They had come out of those planes of consciousness and yet they had forgotten who they were, where they had come from, and the understanding of cosmic law and its outworking. They had even forgotten that they had a mission, that they had made a vow to God to serve the world community. I saw well-meaning parents and teachers at every economic level throughout the nations. And I saw very clearly that they were not able to pass on to their children what they themselves did not know.

There was the dilemma of the centuries, the dilemma of the age, the dilemma of the transition from Pisces to Aquarius. In the midst of the buildup of nuclear power East and West and the uses and abuses of that power in all forms, these were the people who, within their subconscious and superconscious minds, had the key. Yet they were not passing it on because they had forgotten it and no longer knew it at a conscious level.

I was seized with a passion which has never left me, and it

was to go out and find those individuals, wherever they were, and to transfer to them the teaching they had forgotten. I still didn't know what the teaching was. But I knew I was going to get it and I was going to study it, accelerate it, become it and make any sacrifice that was necessary to be worthy of carrying that torch. Then I was going to run with it until those who already had it written in their inward parts would come to know it in their outer awareness.

I also realized clearly that I was not a teacher nor would I ever become a teacher. All I could ever be was a reminder. These were a magnificent people, each one tied to his own God Source. Internally, they knew the Law; I just had to remind them of it. And the moment I would transfer from my heart that light of the Holy Spirit, the ones who knew would be quickened; the ones who did not would not understand. It was as simple as that.

All of this occurred in a few moments of meditation in this higher plane. Then I floated gently back to my body in that little room, and there stood Mark Prophet and he delivered a sermon-lecture. After he finished, I felt his aura increase, probably by the magnitude of ten. The Holy Spirit came upon him. And through the agency of the Holy Spirit came another being of light, an emissary of God. This masterful being would communicate through Mark, by the power of the spoken Word, the message of the Holy Spirit. That being of light was Archangel Michael.

Archangel Michael was standing in the aura of Mark Prophet. The two became congruent, standing in the same point of God-awareness—one in the liberated octaves of Spirit, one in matter. The one in matter was the vessel for the one in Spirit to pour that message of the living God through.

Archangel Michael said many things that night, but what

I noted most was a tremendous power. I saw that the real purpose in the coming of an emissary of God and in the use of the Holy Spirit was not only the transfer of a teaching for our souls and for our consciousness, but it was a transfer of energy, of consciousness. I could feel it entering my chakras.

I knew that there was a spiritual evolution and that this was the purpose of it. There were beings who were just a little bit beyond us in evolution, just beyond the veil of time and space. By their dharma, their duty to become their real selves, they had a supreme obligation to the universe. And that was to pass on that being, that identity, that consciousness to those of lesser evolution.

It is like our obligation when we have a talent that we perfect. If we become skilled in playing the piano, in carpentry or in making flapjacks or if we become a great engineer, surgeon or attorney, we're meant to pass that on to the next person in line. That's how culture moves, that's how civilization moves. This is the order of the universe.

Archangel Michael said, "People of Boston, I'm cutting you free!" I knew he was talking to me, and yet I could feel his light go to every person living in that city. I knew he was cutting me free from whatever it was that was hindering me from finding the ascended master Saint Germain and that mission. It was an answer to a call. It wasn't Saint Germain; it was a means to get to him. And I realized that I myself had to accelerate consciousness until I could be found in a plane of awareness where I could communicate with Saint Germain, and this would be a process.

This was the pivotal event of my life. Everything before it was prologue.

35

The Call

AFTER THAT SERVICE I spent many hours talking with Mark Prophet. Before the night was over I was asking him to teach me how to meditate, how to do whatever the Eastern yogis did. He was tired. He had had a long trip from Washington. But I was so hungry, so desirous to learn.

The next day was Sunday. Ruby Williams, one of the students in Boston, always cooked a meal for the messenger when he came to town, and I was invited to come along. After the meal I asked Mark if I could speak to him. We walked to a little park that was near this home and sat down on a bench. I said to Mark, "I'm supposed to be a messenger."

I had realized this the previous evening when I saw Mark deliver that dictation. It was the first time in my life that I knew my calling, and I knew it mirrored out of the image of Mark Prophet—I saw him and I knew who I was.

I had been reading the "I AM" books, so I knew about messengers. I knew that they delivered dictations from the ascended masters, and I was reading their dictations. But I had no sense of equating myself with a messenger or being a messenger myself. That was the farthest thing from my mind. I was just hoping to become a student of a master—until the fateful day when I met Mark Prophet.

Mark confirmed that it was true. Yes, I was going to be a messenger.

John van Ness, one of the students from Washington, had driven Mark to Boston in his car. At the time, he was Mark's prime financial supporter. His wife was a nurse. I don't know that he worked, but whatever money they had, they gave. They paid for the hall where Mark lectured, and so forth.

On the way back to Washington, Mark told van Ness that I was going to be a messenger. Van Ness said, "If you ever put that woman on the platform, I will withdraw all financial support."

That was probably the first experience I had in the organization of people being against me. He could not stand me on sight. But in spite of all their threatenings, van Ness and his wife did not leave the group. After they got past their initial reaction, they treated me nicely.

SOON MARK SENT me everything he had printed at that time—one or two Keepers of the Flame Lessons, the first three years of the *Pearls of Wisdom,* and a few sheets of decrees. I kept all this locked in a suitcase under my bed in my apartment.

Meanwhile, I attended services in Dr. Whitney's sanctuary, and it wasn't many weeks before I asked him if I could come in and lead a service when they were not holding a regular service there. I wanted to contribute something to the sanctuary and the work of the masters, and I wanted to give decrees for the elementals, the nature spirits.

They gave me a key so I could come in and lead those services. Sometimes I was all alone except for the elementals who gathered for the service. At other times a few of the elderly ladies would come. They had been studying these teachings for many years, but they were very kind and let me lead the service anyway. I had a wonderful time, whether anyone else was present or not.

When Mark returned to Boston at the end of May, I saw him again. I sat at his feet, and every word that came out of his mouth was nourishment to my soul. It was light, it was love. His voice had a gentleness and a caring that I had never heard in my parents. They were not unkind or unloving, but I never heard come out of their mouths the words, the comfort, the teaching or the enlightenment that I received from Mark Prophet. It was as if my soul was parched.

A FEW WEEKS later I was walking through a park to Boston University and a being of light crossed my path. The moment I saw him, I knew him. It was the ascended master El Morya.

He looked almost seven feet tall. His aura was vibrating with a tremendous dedication to the will of God. It was such an impassioned dedication to the will of God that it inspired in me a tremendous trust. It was so impassioned that it became a sternness, almost an abruptness, an intensity of being that one scarcely observes from day to day in people. He looked at me with those intense eyes and said, "I have need of a feminine messenger. Go to Washington and I will train you through Mark Prophet. And if you pass your initiations, Saint Germain will come and anoint you as a messenger for the ascended masters."

It was a cryptic message. That is all he said. He didn't

even wait for an answer and he was off, and I was left standing there. He appeared to me so concretely, looking like any physical person, and yet he was not physical. He had raised my consciousness, cleared my third eye and lowered himself to another plane, and there was a meeting of frequencies in vibrations.

Years later, I went back to Boston and stood on that spot. As I contemplated that experience, I realized that when Morya had appeared to me, he was saying, "You don't have to go by your inner feeling on being a messenger. You don't have to go by a man whom you've just met. I am showing to you and proving to you that the ascended masters are real. I am not asking you to give your life, 100 percent of your life and energy, and to take the ridicule, the scorn and the condemnation of the world for what I am going to pass through you without giving you this initial experience of the absolute integrity and reality of the ascended masters." I saw that he appeared to me out of a sense of cosmic honor, not asking me to walk by faith but by the science of knowing.

IN JULY 1961 I flew down to Washington to attend a Summit Lighthouse conference there. I could scarcely believe what I saw. Through four days of this conference, I saw Mark Prophet deliver dictations from the ascended masters. They were stupendous.

I also saw that Mark Prophet did everything. The couple of days before the class, he was dressed in his overalls and on the floor doing whatever needed to be done to put up the masters' pictures, the flowers, the altar decorations. Then the time would come for the conference and he would bathe, put on his suit or his robe, and he would be on the platform delivering the Word.

Time and again, I saw him just before a dictation and he was bowed down by some situation. Perhaps a group of people from some city were criticizing him, and he had to meet with them and fend off what they were saying. And all of a sudden, the next thing he would be on the platform, his face would be shining, he would be there in his altar robe, and the most stupendous dictations would come forth. And to me, the power of God, the vibration of the dictation and the Word that penetrated my soul was the proof of the messenger and the dispensation, if I ever needed proof. I knew that it was humanly impossible to do what he did. I had never seen a human being do what he did, on the platform and beyond. I saw such tangible radiance of light coming through his skin— it shone with a tremendous light. Whether I was the only one seeing it, I don't know.

In the midst of the phenomenon of seeing Mark Prophet deliver these dictations, a woman at the conference took me to her hotel room and sat me down for two or three hours telling me terrible stories and gossip about Mark. And somehow, it was like it was fed into me and it went into the Christ flame of my heart and was consumed.

Mark had his human idiosyncrasies, which were not the same kind of idiosyncrasies that people had in Red Bank, New Jersey, or in Antioch College or in Boston, Massachusetts. He had Chippewa Falls, Wisconsin, idiosyncrasies, including the accent and the Midwestern twang. And he had the idiosyncrasies of someone who came up through the depression, lived in a small town, didn't finish high school, had been on the spiritual path all his life and was trained as a messenger.

There is no other being I have ever met in this world that was put together like Mark Prophet. And if you weren't ready for that, if you had a preconceived notion about what a messenger should be, how a messenger should be put together and what a messenger should do, say, wear, speak and how he should comport himself—if you didn't get rid of that, you would likely begin to criticize him and begin to finally decide that you knew better than he did and eventually leave the organization.

God always sends prophets and messengers in a peculiar guise. The prophets of Israel were something else to be dealt with. They were absolutely unique in their time and did all kinds of crazy stunts to get the people to obey God's voice. A prophet is someone who goes against the grain of the entire civilization that he comes into. And I think that an out-standing characteristic of the prophet is that he doesn't care what people think of him. He has just come to do a certain thing, he walks with God, and that's it.

I had been looking for this person all my life, and I recognized all of this in Mark Prophet.

36

Beyond Christian Science

AFTER I MET Mark Prophet, I went to see Mr. Carr, my Christian Science teacher. He had come to town on business with the church and I had an appointment to see him. When I arrived, Mr. Carr ushered me into a small sitting area in his hotel room at the Midtown Motor Inn, and I sat down.

I told him about Saint Germain, that I had been studying the "I AM" books, I had found Saint Germain and I had found the messenger of the ascended masters. I went with hope in my heart that he would be broad-minded enough to receive and consider what I was saying. I told him that this was the logical progression from Mary Baker Eddy's teaching. This was the door, this was the next step.

Mr. Carr gave me a long lecture about how this was not true Christian Science. He said that he had explored the "I AM" teachings many years ago and he had cast them aside. They weren't for him. This is where my idol began to crumble.

At the time he was an up-and-coming Christian Scientist and he was going to make a name for himself in Christian

Science. He had become a practitioner and eventually would be a teacher. And what I perceived and the way I interpreted his position was that he was not going to allow anything to compromise his position in the church. He had selected Christian Science as his calling in this life, and if something came along to disturb that, no matter how real or how truthful that something might be, he was not going to have ears to hear, eyes to see or a heart to respond.

I had come to speak with him as my teacher. I put myself before him as his student who had come to discuss the problem of what this was going to mean in my life and for my marriage. I told him the story that I had told Dag before I married him—that when I found Saint Germain I was going to serve him for the rest of my life.

Mr. Carr said, well, I was married now and I should follow my husband, drop out of school and support my husband financially while he was studying. His career was the one that was important and I didn't need to further my education. Regardless of what I had said before I was married, I was married now and I should follow my husband.

As the clincher, and this was supposed to get me to stay in Christian Science, he said, "Betty, odd things happen to people who leave the Christian Science movement." I said, "Like what?" And he said, "Oh, they have accidents, they get killed."

I was so shocked that this came out of his mouth, that he would say this to influence me. And I looked at him and laughed, and I said, "You've got to be kidding. That is absolute superstition," and I would have none of it.

When he was sending me off at the conclusion of the meeting, which he seemed to think went fairly well, he just looked at me, smiled and said, "Betty, burn the books." I felt like saying, "What is this, the Inquisition? I'm supposed to burn the books now?"

So I walked out of that place sadly disillusioned with my teacher. He had not responded to Saint Germain and the "I AM" teachings. He could actually turn his back on these teachings and deny them as real, this my teacher whom I thought had a great light and a great contact with God. This is one of the profound griefs of my life, my disillusionment with my Christian Science teacher.

SINCE THAT TIME, I have reached a new understanding of Christian Science and its teaching. Concluding her treatise set forth in *Science and Health,* Mary Baker Eddy writes of her "present feeble sense of Christian Science."[52] I am sure that none of her students would accuse her of a false humility. Certainly her statement bespeaks the vastness of Christian Science and of the divine science from which it is derived.

If she who healed the sick and cleansed the lepers of their sick sense of self, who cast out the devils of orthodox Christianity and wrote so thoroughly on Christian Science that she established a worldwide religion based on its prin-ciples—if she can call her sense of it "feeble," what are we to call our sense of Christian Science?

I believe that Mrs. Eddy intended her students to follow in her footsteps and even to exceed her, just as Jesus said that those who believe in him should do the works that he did and greater works.[53] Therefore I believe that *Science and Health* and her combined works are written as open books, that in them Mrs. Eddy set forth her present sense of Christian Science and she expected her present feeble sense to yield to a stronger, larger sense in the future. I believe she saw Christian

Science unfolding here and in the hereafter. Moreover, I believe that she expected her students to build on her foundation, which, if feeble, must see the strengthening and enlarging process touching the teaching and the movement from the foundation upward and outward.

I believe that in her concern to protect the growth of the teaching and the movement, however, she fenced in her revelation and left no gate—no way out and no way in.

I believe in the goal for every Christian and every scientist to duplicate the life and work of Jesus and of Mary Baker Eddy—and then to go beyond both to do the greater works that neither one felt satisfied they had achieved in their own lifetime. I believe that the accomplishment of works must be through a path of personal Christhood.

Christian Scientists need to go beyond quoting Jesus and Mary Baker Eddy. They need to internalize the living Word and become that Word in action, become the active force for good in their communities, with signs following.[54] It is not enough to "know the truth"; one must "be the truth" in action.

37

Karma

THE DAY WHEN I heard that Mark Prophet was coming to Boston, I told Dag that I'd like to go to the meeting and I asked him if he would like to go too. He said to me, "You're going to have to choose between me and the ascended masters." And he gave me an ultimatum: "It's either me or Saint Germain." He didn't want me married to him unless I would choose him in place of Saint Germain. That was his ultimatum.

I said, "I have no choice. My mind is already made up, as I told you, and I have to follow Saint Germain." I didn't want to stay married to him on those terms. At that point, Dag moved into the living room and I stayed in the bedroom. The marriage was basically finished.

So then it was a strained relationship. We were going our separate ways, but he didn't quite believe it. He knew that Mark was in the picture in terms of being my teacher. The reason I stayed as long as I did, for four months, was to accrue more credits at B.U. so I could get my degree.

Meanwhile, my parents were trying to discourage me from

following Mark: "This man is a total stranger. He's twice your age. You have no idea who he is, where he came from. What are you doing breaking up your marriage, leaving Christian Science, leaving the Mother Church?" (Mind you, they had never supported me in Christian Science before.)

Every once in a while, I am a bit gullible and a bit naïve, and my parents knew this. I was like that in my teens and in my twenties. So I had to stop and ask myself the same questions they were asking me.

But I just knew I could never go back to Dag. I knew that there was nothing there and that he wouldn't be happy with me anyway. It was an emotional attachment that he had for me. He idealized me. He saw me as a spiritual person. He saw my dedication to Christian Science. And he did not believe I could ever leave that church. He didn't perceive that my devotion was not to the organization but to God himself.

I was called by God, and I knew that this was a true calling. I knew that this was what I had waited for all my life. There was not a shadow of a doubt. I just had to bring up the rear of my emotional body. It was heartbreaking for me to have to end this marriage that I believed in, but I had to go on. I had made this commitment to God.

WHEN I WAS at the 1961 July conference of The Summit Lighthouse in Washington, D.C., I was so burdened and I could not understand how I had married this person to be only married ten months. How did I make this mistake and why did I do it? I begged Mark Prophet to tell me, and finally he relented.

Mark explained to me that when my God Presence said "It is but for a little while," this was telling me that it would be but a little while for the completion of balancing my karma with Dag. Mark explained to me, as he was told by El Morya, that I had karma with this lifestream that had been ongoing for a number of embodiments and I could not become a messenger or be trained to be a messenger until that karma was balanced. Nor could I be contacted by Saint Germain until the karma was balanced. This was why I had sought the master for a number of years before he came.

There is an indelible impression in my being of the memory of the past life with Dag in which I had made this karma, and it was one of the darkest hours of my existence. In the ninth century, I had been born into a family of fishermen in Denmark. When I grew up, a young fisherman was attracted to me, but I was not much interested in him. He went out on a long fishing trip with his father. I can see the ships coming in, and I can see the women and children going to greet these ships and receive their husbands, their fathers and their sons back from the long trip.

I see them coming off the boat and coming up the path. I see the young fisherman coming toward my house. I am in my kitchen and I am preparing a meal. I have a carving knife in my hand and I am cutting up vegetables. He came into my house as I was preparing this meal, and he came at me and he desired me. I rebuffed him, and therefore he raped me. I was outraged. The knife was in my hand, and in my rage at this offense against me, I killed him. This was certainly one of the most tragic events in my history.

I lived this life out, and after I passed on I went before a council of beings of light known as the Lords of Karma. I can remember that scene clearly also. I knelt before them and I was sobbing. I said to them, "I will do anything to balance this karma. I will serve this person as long as you will have me serve him. Let me give him back the life that I took from him." And so the Lords of Karma assigned me to a number of embodiments where I could serve him.

The amazing teaching in this matter is that the crime of murder is not justified by the crime of rape. And we must all remember this when we feel the anger within our souls rise up at the violation of our bodies.

My next lifetime was one of those in which the Lords of Karma graciously gave me the opportunity to balance this karma. I was living in Japan, about A.D. 900. I was born poor, I was forced to marry a man I did not love, and he became a cripple. We lived in abject poverty, eating next to nothing. So I pursued the only trade I could; I became a prostitute, therefore having to voluntarily give my body to many because I had denied it to this one. This man was the same soul I had killed in Denmark. I had to serve him to balance the karma of murder and also to learn the lesson that this body is the body of God, that God will do what he wills with this body and, no matter what, rape does not justify murder.

Eighty years later I returned to Japan again in another embodiment. I was intent on balancing this karma, and the Lords of Karma gave me the opportunity. I was married again to the same man. This time he supported us. He was a taxidermist and I served him as his wife. By the end of that life, the karma of the murder was still not paid off and I had to finish paying it off in this life.

The message from El Morya was that if I had not married Dag and served him, it would have taken me nine years of general service to life to balance that karma. This message conveys the lesson that it is much easier to balance karma with an individual directly, if at all possible. And if the balancing of karma is indirect, it takes longer.

Had I not obeyed this inner voice and married Dag, I would have postponed my meeting of Saint Germain for nine years from that time. And after I met Mark Prophet, it was only twelve years till he took his leave from this octave. So if I had indeed found him nine years later (and I might not have), I would have only had three years with him. Therefore by being obedient to the inner voice and serving this individual, I finished balancing my karma with him.

AFTER THE JULY 1961 conference, I went back home to my apartment in Boston and Dag was there. One night I was in the kitchen preparing a meal and I was cutting vegetables with a large knife. It was a small apartment and Dag was out in the hallway. He started an argument, yelling at me from the hallway, while I was in the kitchen. I forget what the argument was about. Nothing is ever significant about arguments. I think that underneath it all, he was annoyed that I had made the choice for Saint Germain and it was final.

Knife in hand, I walked out into the hallway and started allowing myself to engage in this argument. Then I looked at the knife and I looked at him. In that instant, I dropped the knife, walked back into the kitchen and resumed preparing the meal.

I was so grateful to have had that teaching and to understand that I had come full circle. I was standing at the point where I had been in Denmark with a knife in my hand. And by letting go of the knife, this was the end. I had fulfilled that karma and the relationship ended.

This was a great lesson for me—the fact that karma does limit what we can do in world service, and all of us need to tend to the details of our karma. But when a particular karma is balanced, we have to move on.

After I went to Washington, Dag and I were divorced. I am certain that it was for the better. I haven't been in contact with him since, but I'm sure he's had much greater happiness than he would have if he had remained married to me. So the divorce was the best thing that could have happened.

We didn't divorce over any explosive argument. In fact, we were quite compatible and we were good friends. It was a point of confrontation between two opposing views. I was serving Saint Germain and he was a dedicated Christian Scientist. He didn't want me with that religion and I wasn't going to be deprived of it. There was nothing else to do but for me to leave.

For me, a glimmer of hope in that situation is that the Norwegian name Ytreberg means "the outermost mountain" or "the farthest mountain." I always had the sense that I was destined for that highest mountain. Something else that reflected this glimmer of hope was a tiny diamond that my mother had given to me. When I would be washing dishes and see its light shining underneath the dishwater, it stirred in me tremendous faith that I was on the springboard to Saint Germain. And whatever I was doing, I would do well until he came.

ENTERING THE MARRIAGE with Dag, I walked the tightrope of faith, being entirely blindfolded about what I was actually doing. Now I know that I was fulfilling the requirements to meet Saint Germain, that this was the last labyrinth I had to go through in order to get to meet him. And somehow, my soul just did it.

Sometimes we have to do things that society doesn't approve of. My parents didn't approve of my leaving Dag, my friends didn't approve of it. I had to walk alone to follow Mark Prophet.

Every step of the way, I had to pay the price. And every step up the mountain, there is a price to be paid. If we are willing to pay the price of our karma, step by step we do reach the goal. It is by the sheer grace of God that I was given the opportunity to balance that karma. At inner levels and in many lifetimes, I have asked for the opportunity to balance my karma, and it has never been denied me.

38

Mary

BEFORE I LEFT Boston, I was to have one of the most important experiences on my path. It taught me more about myself than my best instructors and years of philosophy, logic or psychology. I realized that I had had a prejudice imposed upon me since childhood that I had never challenged and never reasoned through for myself. Like anything that we are taught and we accept early in life, it was just there growing inside of me.

Childhood indoctrinations can become such a blindness, such a blight on the natural unfoldment of our souls. Sometimes they are so entrenched that we do not break the stranglehold of our prejudices for decades or even in a given lifetime.

I had always received much comfort in Catholic churches. But I still believed, as I had been told, that Catholics worshiped idols and that Mother Mary was some sort of a goddess who allowed herself to be called the "Mother of God" and other such things. I thought that people worshiped her person in place of God. I didn't understand why a person needed to go through Mary to get to Jesus in order to get to God. And I was taught that people made her equal with or even greater than Jesus Christ or Almighty God himself.

I found myself reacting with intense feelings to the images and icons of Mother Mary all over Boston. One in particular was a huge mural that covered the wall of the subway I took to Boston University every day. On the mural was the title "Queen of the Universe." If she was so great, I thought, why did she allow this blasphemy? I was angry with her. With all the other problems that made for division and confusion in Christendom, why didn't she come down and straighten this one out! I guess I was disturbed only because deep down inside of me I really loved her, and I wanted to know her as she was, as she is, and not as others had portrayed her to me.

That sunny day in Boston, I was in the joy of the presence of God, the hosts of the Lord, the holy angels. They were real. They were moving among us to help us in this "time of trouble" that Daniel foresaw.[55] There was hope, much hope in my heart for the world. Confident in the Lord, I was walking, fairly skipping, along the sidewalk on Commonwealth Avenue in the middle of lunch-hour crowds and traffic. And I was praying and talking to God in joyous realization of his servant sons and daughters, the ascended masters. I had found what I had been looking for.

Yet, though I didn't know it fully, one thing was lacking. One area of my life was still a void. It was in this state of my unawareness, my ignorance, and my conscious and unconscious programmed hostility toward Mary that she found me.

All of a sudden I looked up and there she was! I was face to face with the Blessed Mother. I saw clearly, for the first time in my life, the beautiful Mary, a being of great light. A charge of light and indescribable joy passed through my body, traveling like a loop of electricity from my head to my feet and back again. I remember the exact place in the pavement where I was stopped—transfixed, transformed.

She had the face of a young maiden, a daughter of God. She was Michelangelo's *Pietà,* alive and well and glorious. I saw her at once as Mary, the Woman of the age, and as a light emanation of a greater light. Her immaculate heart was on fire with an energy that she transmitted at will to me, to anyone. It was clear that she was the one whose pure devotion to the Father was a crystal stream, and its issue was the Son, Jesus Christ.

There she was before me, the most transcendent and lovely young woman, full of grace, truth, beauty and integrity. She was suspended above and before me, as real as you are, as real as I am. She was someone you could invite into your kitchen to have a cup of tea, someone you could talk to about anything. She was someone just like me, except that she was in another dimension.

But she wasn't quite like me; she was something much more. Her presence was resplendent with the light she had adored and become. She had become something of a cosmos all her own. She had entered into and consciously become a part of life, infinity, that I had not. She had realized a greater portion of the Self than most of earth's evolutions had any idea even existed. There was enough like her (the divine part) in me, and enough like me (the human part) in her that I knew that whatever she had done to become what she was, I could follow her lead and do it, too, if she would show me the way.

The love of her heart poured out to me. It melted my soul,

my self. In the presence of her immense compassion, I was being wrapped in the swaddling garment of her understanding. She knew my sin and understood it. There was an exchange. By her wisdom I was made whole. In that instant I realized that I had loved her, the real Mother Mary, forever.

All of that unreal overlay from earlier years dropped from me, and I saw her in all of her beauty, radiance, love and utter humility before God—and before his light burning in my own being, however imperfect. I felt ashamed that I had allowed myself to be shrouded in the world's consciousness covering the Mother. And I thought, "What other brainwashing have you accepted because it is the way of the world? Think of it! All of this you have taken in from other people contrary to your truest feelings, and from people who have set themselves up as authorities in matters of the soul in its communion with the Spirit. This you were willing to accept—without going to the fount of Life and demanding your own empirical, scientifically spiritual proof—when Life as God, as Mother was so ready and willing to reveal itself to you!"

I was so moved and so touched by her reality, instead of the unreality that I had been programmed to feel, that I literally ran to the nearest Catholic church. I knelt before her statue and asked for forgiveness for the negative thoughts and feelings I had held. I also gave to her my life and asked her to use me as an instrument of her mothering of all people.

Ever since then, the joy that I've had of having Mother Mary as a constant companion and adviser in my life has been simply boundless. I am so grateful that Mother Mary was concerned enough about one person to show me her presence and her reality. Instantaneously, this dissolved all of a lifetime's worth of indoctrination. I realized that if she had not done this, I would not have had that conversion of the Holy

Spirit she conveyed and I would have been left in ignorance. I would have been left in a state of making the karma of disputing the office, presence and person of this one who serves as the Blessed Mother.

In knowing Mary as she truly is, I have come to see her as a relentless and constant force, challenging the oppression of her children everywhere, in every faith, in every religion. She is a World Mother, and I have seen this in her tremendous mastery of life.

Even in my willfulness and independence, God was showing me little by little how utterly and totally inadequate my subjective awareness was. I was being shown and I was coming to accept, with a newfound humility and patience, that I desperately needed a teacher.

39

A New Life

EL MORYA APPEARED to me one more time before I left Boston to go to Washington, D.C. He gave me one more proof, because he knew the element of doubt that lurks within all of us, and sure enough it was lurking.

I was in my apartment preparing to pass the torch in various college organizations and at work, and I was trying to get my things together. It seemed like a tall order to get all of this done and leave.

Suddenly, I felt him come through the door of the apartment, although, of course, he didn't need to come through the door. He stood there big and tall, vibrating with the momentum of his devotion to the will of God. The doubting part of me said, "Go ahead and prove he's not real! Go ahead! Just step through him. If you can step through him, he's not real." And I thought, "Well, that makes sense."

So there he stood in front of me with a love that is indescribable, with the intensity of the devotion to my soul and to everything I had ever been seeking. But in that split second I made a decision. I walked through him. I walked

233

right through him, and I turned around and he was still there. I then felt very sheepish and very embarrassed. I had proven nothing except that the ascended masters are real.

Morya was real. He stayed with me. Things got together and I was ready to go.

But I had that last moment of looking back, that great sin of Lot's wife. And it was a looking back because I was leaving my family and everyone I knew in church, in school and on the job. In fact, I was walking out on my whole life without even being able to communicate to anyone why I was leaving. I knew that they wouldn't understand and there was no point in even beginning the discussion. I was just leaving town, and I was saying, "Good-bye, I am going."

In the face of all this, there was a horrendous outcry, and it began to be a pull, like the pull of a planet. Everybody I knew was pulling on me. It was such a magnetism that I couldn't leave. I was walking out of my church, walking out of my marriage, walking out of my entire life to follow one man that I'd seen only a few times. Everybody was in an uproar. My parents were furious and automatically hated this man, who was twenty years older than me.

The energy was extremely heavy and I didn't think I was going to be able to get through it. But every time I had ever had a problem, I would open my Bible and Jesus would give me the verse I needed to read. So I said, "Jesus, I know this is the will of God. You want me to do this. I need the strength and I need the direction." And the Bible fell open, and it said, "There were two laborers laboring in the field. One was taken and another was left."

And so I said, "I understand. He can't go along." For reasons unknown to me, I was the one taken, and that statement gave me the light and the courage I needed and on I went.

I HAD RECEIVED letters addressed to me from Morya and Saint Germain telling me to come to Washington. I had the visions of Morya in the park and in my apartment. The signals were clear. I had all the indicators that told me I must go. Whatever it would cost me, I must go. And I wanted to go. I had found my teacher. I had found Saint Germain. I was ready.

It was not a minute too soon, but it was also not a minute too late. The ascended masters let me mature, which included the experience of being married and balancing that karma. They let me be my own guru until it was obvious to me that I needed a Guru.

I had rough places in my personality from my own karma, my own past embodiments and from the example of my parents. And I was extremely strong willed. Growing up in a small town in the East and going to school in New England, I had a certain attitude. Mark Prophet grew up in Wisconsin and hadn't finished high school. And between me and Mark, there was a twenty-year age difference. Given that the human will is unpredictable, the masters couldn't predict what might happen when we got together.

Would I reject him because of this or that human idiosyncrasy he had? Or would I have hungered and longed for the masters so long that when I finally found him, I would be ready?

The latter was the case. I was definitely ready.

ON AUGUST 23, 1961, Mark came to my apartment in Boston and moved me out. He, Dag and I moved my furniture, my clothes, my books and all of my belongings into a U-Haul that was attached to the back of Mark's car. When we were finished packing, I kissed Dag good-bye, walked out with Mark, got in the car, and started the long journey to Washington, D.C.

When I walked out of that apartment, it was like I had concluded one lifetime and I was starting another. It was so sudden. I cried most of the way to Washington. It was a very traumatic experience.

But I knew I wanted to do it. I was absolutely certain I wanted to do it.

So that evening in Washington, I knelt at my bed and called to El Morya. I had his framed picture right on my bed. I said, "El Morya, I know that by tomorrow morning all of this is going to be gone." I had the absolute conviction that's exactly what was going to happen. "El Morya, I know you're going to take this from me," I said, "and tomorrow my training will start, and I'm going to do it."

I got up the next morning. There was not even a hint of any burden. I was ready for my mission.

Elizabeth Clare Prophet

Chronology

April 8, 1939   Born at Monmouth Memorial Hospital, Long Branch, N.J.

March 3, 1942   Hans Wulf taken to Ellis Island

September 1944   Starts school

Spring 1946   Trip to Switzerland to visit relatives

Summer 1948   Leg injury keeps her in bed the whole summer

1949   Jane Petherbridge moves to Maine

July 1949   Summer camp at Camp Matollionequay

June 1952   Travels to Maine with her mother to visit Jane Petherbridge; visits Boston on the way home

July 1953   Spends a month with Jane Petherbridge

Summer 1954   Jane Petherbridge visits Red Bank and Beach Haven

June 1955   Attends Red Bank High senior prom with Vladimir

Summer 1955   Visits Beach Haven alone

April 8, 1956   Prompting from Saint Germain to go to Switzerland to study French

May 28, 1956   Leaves for Switzerland

July 1956   Starts high school in Neuchâtel

December 1956	Visits Paris on the way home from Switzerland
January 1957	Commences final half of senior year in high school at Red Bank High
June 1957	Graduates from high school
Summer 1957	Summer job as a waitress
September 1957	Sees picture of Saint Germain
	Commences studies at Antioch College
Summer 1958	French summer camp at École Champlain
August 6, 1958	Letter to Godfré Ray King
August 7, 1958	Founding of The Summit Lighthouse
Fall 1958	Assistant to delegates' photographer at the Thirteenth General Assembly of the United Nations
Winter 1959	Final quarter at Antioch College
Spring 1959	Co-op job at Tufts University
May 1959	Meets Charles M. Carr
August 1959	Attends Christian Science class instruction with Mr. Carr at Montclair, N.J.
September 1959	Commences classes at Boston University
	Works at *Christian Science Monitor*
May 1960	Marries Dag Ytreberg
September 1960	Starts teaching at Christian Science Mother Church Sunday school
April 22, 1961	Meets Mark Prophet
June 1961	Called by El Morya to go to Washington, D.C., to be trained as a messenger
July 1961	Attends Summit Lighthouse conference in Washington
August 1961	Moves to Washington to commence her training to be a messenger for the ascended masters

Notes

All quotes from the Bible are taken from the King James Version.

1. I Cor. 13:11, 12.
2. The ascended masters are enlightened spiritual beings who once lived on earth, fulfilled their reason for being and have ascended, or reunited with God. The ascended masters are the true teachers of mankind. They direct the spiritual evolution of all devotees of God and guide them back to their Source.
3. The Great Commandment: "Thou shalt love the Lord thy God with all thy heart, and with all thy soul, and with all thy mind. This is the first and great commandment. And the second is like unto it, Thou shalt love thy neighbor as thyself." Matt. 22:37–39.
4. The astral plane is the lowest vibrating frequency of time and space; the repository of mankind's thoughts and feelings, conscious and unconscious.
5. Mark 10:27.
6. John 5:17.
7. Mary Baker Eddy, *Science and Health with Key to the Scriptures* (Boston: First Church of Christ, Scientist, 1971), p. 468.
8. Exod. 20:3.
9. Matt. 6:24.
10. Mary Baker Eddy, "Feed My Sheep," 1887.
11. The collective subconscious of the planet has been described by the ascended masters as the astral sea. Souls departing this earth must navigate through these realms of darkness and illusion in order to reach the octaves of light known as the etheric plane.
12. Rev. 16:7.
13. William Shakespeare, "Sonnet 30," lines 13–14.

14. Matt. 22:37; Deut. 6:5.
15. Kahlil Gibran, *The Prophet* (New York: Alfred A. Knopf, 1953), p. 12.
16. Heb. 12:6.
17. Mark 10:29, 30.
18. Matt. 28:18.
19. I Cor. 13:7.
20. I Cor. 12–14.
21. Isa. 1:18.
22. I Cor. 13:10.
23. Matt. 10:37.
24. Ps. 23:4.
25. John 11:25.
26. I John 4:8, 16.
27. Mary Baker Eddy, "Communion Hymn."
28. Jer. 31:33; Heb. 10:16.
29. John 6:53.
30. Exod. 3:14.
31. John 6:35; 8:12; 10:7, 11; 11:25; 14:6; 15:5.
32. John 10:30; 5:30; 14:10; 5:17; 9:4.
33. John 14:12.
34. Phil. 2:5.
35. Mary Baker Eddy, "Tenets of the Mother Church," first tenet, in *Manual of the Mother Church* (Boston: Trustees under the Will of Mary Baker G. Eddy, 1936), p. 15.
36. Luke 2:19.
37. Mary Baker Eddy, *Science and Health*, p. 308.
38. Ibid., p. 577.
39. Rev. 7:9–17.
40. Mary Baker Eddy, *Science and Health*, p. 513 (italics mine).
41. Ibid., p. 476 (italics mine).
42. Ibid., pp. 264–65 (italics mine).
43. For example, see Irving C. Tomlinson, *Twelve Years with Mary Baker Eddy: Recollections and Experiences* (Boston: Christian Science Publishing Society, 1945).
44. Mary Baker Eddy, *Christ and Christmas: A Poem*, stanza 12 (Boston: Trustees under the Will of Mary Baker G. Eddy, 1925), p. 53.
45. Ps. 148:1–5.
46. Luke 2:13.
47. Hymn by Arthur C. Ainger, "Purpose."
48. Years later when I was studying the Teachings of the Ascended Masters, I learned that Archangel Gabriel is the angel of the annunciation, not only to Mary and Joseph announcing the birth of the Christ Child but to all mothers and fathers who are to bring forth a child, even though they may not be aware of the angel's presence. I also learned that Archangel Gabriel comes to announce key initiations in the

life of the soul. Thus I realized that it was Gabriel himself whose presence I felt on the church steps and who put the words in my mouth, "Why, I have to make my ascension in this life!"

49. Mary Baker Eddy, *Science and Health*, p. 581.
50. John 10:16.
51. When I came to understand the teachings of the masters, I realized that Matter is real in the sense that it is the repository for Spirit—it is a chalice. It is not hard and dense, but it is energy in motion. Matter really is Mother, and it is the polarity of Spirit. But most of it is illusion; most of it is unreal. Most of what we see as Matter is maya.

But the greater understanding I received from the masters is that Spirit and Matter are not two distinct things, but they are one, as the totality of God's wholeness. And when we look at ourselves, at what appears to be Matter, we are actually seeing Spirit coalesced in form. Some of what we see isn't real, and some of what we see is real. And so it depends on the way you conceive of the words whether you would say "Matter is not real," or "Matter is real."

52. Mary Baker Eddy, *Science and Health*, p. 577.
53. John 14:12.
54. Mark 16:20.
55. Dan. 12:1.

FOR MORE INFORMATION

Summit University Press books are available at fine bookstores worldwide and at your favorite online bookseller.

For a free catalog of our books and products or for information about seminars and conferences, please contact:

Summit University Press
63 Summit Way, Gardiner, MT 59030-9314 USA
Tel: 1-800-245-5445 or 406-848-9500
Fax: 1-800-221-8307 or 406-848-9555

E-mail: info@SummitUniversityPress.com
www.SummitUniversityPress.com
www.SummitLighthouse.org
www.MysticalPaths.org
www.PocketGuidesToPracticalSpirituality.com
www.SummitLighthouse.org/iTunes.html
www.YouTube.com/TheSummitLighthouse
www.ElizabethClareProphet.org

ELIZABETH CLARE PROPHET is a world-renowned author, lecturer and teacher who has pioneered techniques in practical spirituality, including the creative power of sound for personal growth and world transformation. Among her best-selling books are *Fallen Angels and the Origins of Evil*, *The Lost Years of Jesus*, The Lost Teachings of Jesus series, *Kabbalah: Key to Your Inner Power* and her Pocket Guides to Practical Spirituality series, which includes *Creative Abundance* and *Violet Flame to Heal Body, Mind and Soul*.

For almost three decades Elizabeth Clare Prophet provided leadership for The Summit Lighthouse and the Keepers of the Flame Fraternity, both founded by her late husband Mark L. Prophet. Together they established Summit University in 1971. Four years later Mrs. Prophet founded Church Universal and Triumphant and Summit University Press. More than one hundred of their books have been published by Summit University Press and a wide selection of them are translated into a total of twenty-nine languages. They are the world and from online booksellers.

During her career Mrs. Prophet taught in more than thirty countries worldwide, conducting seminars and retreats on such topics as karma and reincarnation, angels, prophecy and the mystical paths of the world's religions.

Mrs. Prophet retired in 1999 for health reasons and is now living in Montana's Rocky Mountains. The works of Mark L. Prophet and Elizabeth Clare Prophet continue to be published by Summit University Press.

Printed in the United States
132815LV00002B/2/P